C000065285

THE NORTH EAST AFTER BREXIT

BREXIT STUDIES SERIES

Series Editors: Alex De Ruyter, Jon Yorke and Haydn Davies, Centre for Brexit Studies, Birmingham City University, UK

With the vote on 23 June 2016 for the UK to leave the European Union it has become imperative for individuals, business, government and wider society to understand the implications of the referendum result. This series, published in collaboration with the Centre for Brexit Studies at Birmingham City University, UK, examines a broad sweep of topics related to Brexit. It aims to bring together academics from across the disciplines to confront and examine the challenges withdrawal from the EU brings. The series promotes rigorous engagement with the multifaceted aspects of both the 'leave' and 'remain' perspectives in order to enhance understanding of the consequences for the UK, and for its relationship with the wider world, of Brexit, and aims to suggest measures to counter the challenges faced.

Previously Published

David Hearne and Alex de Ruyter, *Regional Success After Brexit: The Need for New Measures*

Stefania Paladini and Ignazio Castellucci, *European Security in a Post-Brexit World*

Alex de Ruyter and Beverly Nielsen, *Brexit Negotiations After Article 50*

Forthcoming titles

Arantza Gomez Arana, *Brexit and Gibraltar: The Negotiations of a Historically Contentious Region*

THE NORTH EAST AFTER BREXIT

Impact and Policy

EDITED BY

JOYCE LIDDLE

AND

JOHN SHUTT

United Kingdom – North America – Japan – India
Malaysia – China

Emerald Publishing Limited
Howard House, Wagon Lane, Bingley BD16 1WA, UK

First edition 2020

Editorial matter and selection © 2020 Joyce Liddle and John Shutt,
published under exclusive licence. Individual chapters © 2020
the respective authors

Reprints and permissions service
Contact: permissions@emeraldinsight.com

No part of this book may be reproduced, stored in a retrieval
system, transmitted in any form or by any means electronic,
mechanical, photocopying, recording or otherwise without
either the prior written permission of the publisher or a licence
permitting restricted copying issued in the UK by The Copyright
Licensing Agency and in the USA by The Copyright Clearance
Center. No responsibility is accepted for the accuracy of
information contained in the text, illustrations or advertisements.
The opinions expressed in these chapters are not necessarily
those of the Author or the publisher.

British Library Cataloguing in Publication Data
A catalogue record for this book is available from the British
Library

ISBN: 978-1-83909-012-7 (Print)
ISBN: 978-1-83909-009-7 (Online)
ISBN: 978-1-83909-011-0 (Epub)

Printed and bound by CPI Group (UK) Ltd, Croydon, CR0 4YY

ISOQAR certified
Management System,
awarded to Emerald
for adherence to
Environmental
standard
ISO 14001:2004.

Certificate Number 1985
ISO 14001

INVESTOR IN PEOPLE

CONTENTS

PART I
THE IMPACTS OF DEVOLUTION ON
THE NORTH EAST

PART II
THE IMPACTS OF BREXIT AND KEY
POLICY AREAS

PART III
NEW STRATEGIES FOR PUBLIC SECTOR
CHANGE: CROSSING BOUNDARIES

LIST OF FIGURES AND BOXES

FIGURES

BOXES

LIST OF TABLES

ABOUT THE EDITORS

Professor Joyce Liddle is a Professor of Public Leadership and Enterprise, Director of Research and Innovation at Newcastle Business School, Northumbria University. She was previously Professor of Public Leadership and Management at IMPGT, Aix-Marseille Université and is a graduate of the Universities of Durham and Warwick.

Professor John Shutt is a Professor of Public Policy and Management at Newcastle Business School, Northumbria University. He is a graduate of Leeds Beckett, Birmingham and Cardiff Universities. He was previously a Visiting Professor at the College of Business and Management at Zhejiang University of Technology (ZJUT) in Hangzhou, China.

John and Joyce are working together at Newcastle Business School to establish and lead research and teaching in Public Sector Policy and Management.

LIST OF CONTRIBUTORS

Professor Ignazio Cabras, Professor in Entrepreneurship and Regional Economic Development, Newcastle Business School, Northumbria University, UK

Professor David Charles, Professor of Enterprise and Innovation, Newcastle Business School, Northumbria University, UK

Professor James A. Cunningham, Professor of Strategy Management and Director of Research and Innovation, Entrepreneurship, Innovation and Strategy, Newcastle Business School, Northumbria University, UK

Dr Ian C. Elliott, Senior Lecturer, Newcastle Business School, Northumbria University, UK

Dr. Martyn Griffin, Associate Professor, Durham University Business School, UK

Dr Nicola Headlam, Head of Northern Powerhouse, Cities and Local Growth Unit, BEIS and Treasury, UK

Mr David Jamieson, Postgraduate Associate, Newcastle Business School, Northumbria University, UK

Dr Lorraine Johnston, Senior Lecturer, Newcastle Business School, Northumbria University, UK

Professor Joyce Liddle, Professor of Public Leadership and Enterprise, Director, Research and Innovation, HR and Leadership, Newcastle Business School, Northumbria University, UK

Professor Mike Martin, Chair of Enterprise Information Sciences, Newcastle Business School, Northumbria University, UK

Professor John Mawson, Director of Institute for Local Governance (ILG), Durham Business School, Durham University, UK

Professor Tom Mordue, Professor of Tourism and Head of School for Entrepreneurship, Newcastle Business School, Northumbria University, UK

Dr Debbie Porteous, Associate Professor, Department of Nursing, Midwifery and Health, Northumbria University, UK

Dr Michele Rusk, Associate Professor of Innovation & Entrepreneurial Leadership, Newcastle Business School, UK

Professor Keith Shaw, Professor of Politics, Faculty of Art and Design and Social Sciences, Northumbria University, UK

Professor John Shutt, Professor of Public Policy and Management, Newcastle Business School, UK

Professor John Wilson, Dean and PVC, Newcastle Business School, Northumbria University, UK

Professor Rob Wilson, Professor of Digital Business, Newcastle Business School, Northumbria University, UK

FOREWORD

Northumbria University is now a Top 50 British University with a research and a teaching mission rooted in helping the North and the regional economy to transform and develop a more competitive base that will provide a better future.

The challenges of this task have always been daunting, as anyone who understands the history of this North East region of the United Kingdom will relate. The coal, iron and steel industries shaped the region, together with shipbuilding and heavy engineering and chemicals, and this complex industrial past still matters. Many of the advanced manufacturing industries of today have evolved from this history and traditions. However, since the 1930s onwards regional and urban policies have sought to transform and modernise the region and encourage growth in new industries through inward investment and the indigenous growth of small firms.

The challenges of regional and city development and of regional governance and devolution and leadership are at the heart of debates about how best to advance the interests of the region in a global economy, and how best to respond to Brexit and build and secure employment in the advanced industries of the future. The academic team at Newcastle Business School presented here is at the forefront of regional and public policy debates nationally and internationally. The contributors to the chapters in this timely manuscript argue that there needs to be a much greater focus on place, leadership and the role of the region in global and European economies.

Policies are constantly changing, and now we must deal with the Brexit moment. In recent years, we have seen the Regional Development Agencies replaced by the Local Enterprise Partnerships and the North East LEP is leading the way with its Strategic Economic Plan, in response to Brexit and now the new local industrial strategy. The new devolved Combined Authorities for the North of the Tyne and Tees Valley and now the rise of the Northern Powerhouse: both demand new ways of working, as well as an imperative for North East leaders to collaborate with their North West and Yorkshire and the Humber counterpart regions by working more closely together.

In this complex arena, Universities and Business Schools are focussing on both their Civic University roles and missions, and on Knowledge Exchange priorities for graduate employment and community and social and environmental development. More multidisciplinary research is required to shed a spotlight on some of the most challenging problems, whether in housing and social policy or health, transport and in energy and climate change. Greater evaluation is required of the effectiveness of existing programmes and evidence-based research must be at the forefront of policy initiatives. Recent debates have focussed on the role of Civic Universities in transforming the United Kingdom in the decade ahead, and on the specific importance of Business Schools and Universities in an age of increasing uncertainty.

Northumbria's mission is to join the Top 30 UK universities in research leadership and to play a leading role in the future of regional economic development in the North East. The essays presented here are designed to help people inside and out with the region to think through some of the key drivers of change which we face as the next decade approaches, and to present up-to-date analysis of what more needs to change if the region is to alter its path of development and take greater advantage of the devolution process.

Whether it is the Industrial Strategy, Enterprise Zones, Free Ports or the new 'Strength in Places' or 'Shared Prosperity' Funds, Newcastle Business School and Northumbria University intend to be at the heart of modern public policy debate, and will continue to work alongside its key stakeholders in the public, private and third sectors across the region to understand how we might better boost competitive advantage in the North East over the coming decade.

Professor John Wilson
Pro Vice-Chancellor (Business and Law),
Northumbria University, UK
November 2019

PART I

THE IMPACTS OF DEVOLUTION ON THE NORTH EAST

1

AN UNDERPOWERED NORTHERN POWERHOUSE: INFRASTRUCTURE IN THE UNGOVERNABLE NORTH[1]

Nicola Headlam

Much like English grammar – English devolution is all exception and no rule.

Is it going to be a Strategic strategy? Or – y'know, the other kind?

INTRODUCTION: A CRISIS FAST AND SLOW

Fundamental questions of constitutional structures, centre-region relations, institutional co-ordination and public expenditure ... are addressed as the perhaps unglamorous dimensions of sub-national government and governance. (Pike & Tomaney, 2004, p. 249

3

> *Some of the most radical changes to the globalizing*
> *world are being written, not in the language of*
> *law and diplomacy, but rather in the language of*
> *infrastructure space. Massive global infrastructure*
> *systems, administered by mixtures of public*
> *and private cohorts and driven by profound*
> *irrationalities, generate de facto, undeclared forms*
> *of polity faster than any even quasi-official forms of*
> *governance can legislate them. (Easterling, 2014)*

FIVE YEARS OF THE NORTHERN POWERHOUSE AND THE DEVELOPMENT OF TRANSPORT FOR THE NORTH

The Northern Powerhouse across the three Northern regions is a diverse and innovative economy, representing a shared commitment to delivering good jobs in a wider Northern region that takes pride in its industrial heritage and its natural capital. Government is delivering on this commitment through: focussing on maximising connectivity across the North; supporting innovation, seeking greater levels of research and development (R&D) and strategically important industries; and emphasising the centrality of clean and inclusive growth to our future prosperity (Box 1.1).

> *We will ensure cities, towns and more rural areas*
> *all contribute to a Northern Powerhouse that trades*
> *successfully as a highly-productive economy with*
> *partners around the world.*

The North of England was the first region in Europe to industrialise. It led the world in manufacturing, extraction and international trade. Numerous cities and towns grew exponentially across the North, pulled by national and global demand and

Box 1.1. The Northern Powerhouse Brand.

THE TIME TO INVEST IS NOW

Building a Northern Powerhouse is about boosting the local economy by investing in skills, innovation, transport and culture, as well as devolving significant powers and budgets to directly elected mayors to ensure decisions in the North are made by the North. We are backing business growth right across the North, and giving our great cities the power and resources they need to reach their huge untapped potential.

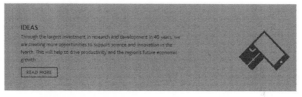

IDEAS

Through the largest investment in research and development in 40 years, we are creating more opportunities to support science and innovation in the North. This will help to drive productivity and the region's future economic growth.

READ MORE

INFRASTRUCTURE

We are driving forward the biggest investment in the North for a generation and are committed to improving everyday journeys, developing skills and rolling out superfast broadband to deliver the improvements that the region needs for the long term.

READ MORE

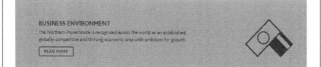

BUSINESS ENVIRONMENT

The Northern Powerhouse is recognised across the world as an established, globally competitive and thriving economic area with ambition for growth.

READ MORE

Source: BEIS – https://northernpowerhouse.gov.uk/

pushed by the talents and energy of its people. Yet in the North's historic strengths were also the seeds of future problems. Technological and market change left capital and people intensive industries behind. Linkages between cities and other forms of settlement which had grown up around a single industry lost purpose and linkages with prosperity as traditional industries declined. The multiplicity of municipal actors across the north made it difficult to develop coherent strategies for the north. And policy-makers in London lost track of the North's needs.

THE NORTHERN POWERHOUSE 2014–2019

Now, we want the North to be attractive again to global investors and to develop a positive balance of trade with the rest of the world as a region once again characterised as an export giant. We also want the North to be a place where people choose to move to, to build careers and bring up families.

Officials have been developing proposals for a cross-government strategy that clearly demonstrates government's commitment to the North of England. As the Industrial Strategy for the North, the Northern Powerhouse Strategy should set a new ambitious plan for growth in the Northern Powerhouse as we leave the European Union (EU).

This vision is a shared ambition developed with key civic leaders, businesses, Local Enterprise Partnerships and communities across the North for better places. It Includes opportunities driven by a new hybrid quango – Transport for the North (TfN) – around Northern Powerhouse Rail (NPR), with strategically supported industries and a focus on clean growth. It identifies opportunities to maximise the North's natural capital and quality of life to the heart of a thriving and innovative economy that delivers good jobs and prosperity to its residents, and productivity-led growth for the North and the rest of the country. As we look to leave the European Union, these connections will become even more important to build on the brand and recognition of the Northern Powerhouse to the international community.

As the recent 'Power up the North' campaign by northern newspapers and associated engagement shows, there is a working consensus among northern stakeholders about what is required to mend decades of underinvestment in the North's economy. We think the strategy will need to address this head on, with success measured regionally in these relatively headline terms.

The 'Power up the North' campaign asks:

- Deliver a fundamental shift in decision-making out of London, giving devolved powers and self-determination to people in the north.

- Commit funding immediately to make NPR a national priority.

- Overhaul the region's road and rail network as a part of a wider environmental plan, with devolved funding and powers.

- Put full weight behind a bespoke Industrial Strategy for the North of England to enable every sector of the economy, from manufacturing to farming, to flourish.

- Make additional investment available for the North's schools, colleges and universities to boost skills training.

- Set out a programme to build a new generation of social housing and affordable homes.

- Accelerate investment in the north's digital infrastructure, particularly in rural areas, and support creative industries.

- Commit that the government's 'shared prosperity fund', intended to replace EU structural funding after 2014–2020, to be fully devolved in long-term tranches to enable strategic decisions of scale rather than areas having to bid in for smaller amounts, piecemeal.

- Elevate the post of Northern Powerhouse minister to Cabinet status, with full powers, as a clear signal that government intends to take the Northern Powerhouse seriously.

A refreshed Northern Powerhouse strategy which does not address these issues will lack credibility with all the regional stakeholders. In order to face the challenges of the knowledge society in the North we recommend consolidating the foundations of productivity and the Grand Challenges from the modern Industrial Strategy with the jointly developed priorities emerging from the new northern Local Industrial Strategies into three strands of activity:

- Northern strengths ideas, business environment, people;

- Northern links connectivity, infrastructure and the future of mobility;

- Northern places making and shaping places for people through devolved and new pan-Northern institutions.

THE NORTHERN POWERHOUSE: A PRODUCTIVITY AND PERFORMANCE LAG

TfN's Northern Powerhouse Independent Economic Review (NPIER) outlines the gaps in productivity and performance between the Northern Powerhouse when compared to London, the rest of England and comparator regions internationally. This gap widened, rather than narrowed between the early 2000s and 2013.

The North falls behind the rest of England on its 'performance', as measured by gross value added (GVA) per capita. For the last 30 years the North has been around 25% behind the rest of the England and 10–15% behind the rest of England minus London. This gap widened, rather than narrowed between the early 2000s and 2013.

The primary drivers of this performance gap are productivity and employment gaps between the North and the rest of the country. When London is considered, the productivity gap accounted for more of the difference, indicating that the North has fewer people in work and fewer people earning high wages that the rest of England, with the wage gap being most significant when London is considered in the comparison group. Lower costs in the North account for only around 3–4% of the difference.

Though these differences are stark, the closing of them represents an opportunity for the North. 'The Northern Powerhouse: One Agenda, One Economy, One North Report' found that if the North's GVA grew in line with the rest of England it would represent a real-terms boost to the economy of £37bn. TfN's NPIER lays out a transformational scenario that assumes substantial sector growth in the North's four prime capabilities of advanced manufacturing, energy, digital, health innovation and three enabling capabilities of financial and professional services, logistics and Higher education. This means 850,000 additional jobs compared with 'business as usual'.

Analyses abound on the specificities of the economic challenges for the Northern Powerhouse. In 2016 the Northern Powerhouse, grew at an annual real rate of 0.5%, considerably lower than the previous year's growth of 2.6%, with the North East region actually contracting by –1% and the Yorkshire and the Humber region showing no growth over 2016 (ONS); GVA per hour worked in the Northern Powerhouse has consistently been over 10% lower than the England average between 2004 and 2015 (the latest available data). In 2015, GVA per hour worked was 15% lower in the Northern Powerhouse, compared to the England average. Further recent figures from the Department of International Trade (DIT) show across the north, reductions in foreign direct investment. Treasury analysis shows that EU exit effects may disproportionately affect the Midlands and the North because they are the most EU-dependent and least-diversified local economies outside of London and the South East.

For the North of England, it is completely congruent with international experience that the existence of TfN, as a new statutory transportation entity, has many of the characteristics of experimental forms of governance within and out – with major cities which are seeking to leverage investment for infrastructure.

It is through the financialisation of infrastructure spending where these hybrid forms are emerging and where recombination's of power, authority and spending are being configured across markets and bureaucracies with unpredictable and possibly unstable quango's emerging as the preferred governing mode.

A CONTEXT OF INCREASING UNCERTAINTIES

Such tangles require more robust institutions and empowered professionals able to exercise judgements and make decisions. Not ambivalence and a polity characterised by diffusion from above and below within a multi-actor and multi-level polity which is too fragmented and weak. The essential contingency and complexity of governance construction, however sees actors pulled not only from the National Centre but also regionally and supra-regionally (vertically from above). There are those more convinced by an approach emphasising meta-governance or controlling government from higher spatial scales.

Wicked issues: There is no definitive formula of a wicked problem. Wicked problems have no stopping rule. Solutions for wicked problems are not rule-false or good-bad. There is no immediate test of a solution to a wicked problem. Every solution to a wicked problem is a 'one-shot' operation because there is no opportunity to learn by trial and error, every attempt counts significantly.

Wicked problems do not have an enumerable set of potential solutions nor is there a well-described set of permissible operations that may be incorporated into to plan. Every wicked problem is essentially unique. Every wicked problem can be a symptom of another problem. The existence of a discrepancy representing a wicked problem can be explained in numerous ways, but the planner has no right to be wrong.

Despite the lack of 'glamour' associated with the specificities of sub-national governing, this chapter seeks to connect the polity-forming criteria above from the work of Pike and Tomaney, with the work on the informal 'de facto, undeclared' forms of governance that engineer and enable 'infrastructure space'. It seeks to frame the current Brexit moment within the turbulence of the 'slow crisis' of the economic separating the regions of England, in the context of the 'fast crisis' of the consequences of EU Exit, and it seeks to help people think about where we want to take the Northern Powerhouse brand and set of concepts in the decade ahead.

THINKING ABOUT THE NORTHERN POWERHOUSE

I argue that it is possible to approach the peculiarities of the Northern Powerhouse as an interactive and dynamic policy space populated by overlapping layers and cliques of actors who animate the governance space by wielding technologies of governance of brand, plan and strategy.

In work focussing on the construction and circulation of myths about city-regional institution building, the properties of the actors engaged in the governing work of constructing and maintaining a regime falls into three discrete types:

(1) Politicians and bureaucrats, officials of mandated central and local and European government entities.

(2) What I call the Qualgae, quasi-local governance actors and institutions and entities populated by policy entrepreneurs (Mintrom & Norman, 2009) and pragmatic localists (Coaffee & Headlam, 2008) who I call 'Qualgecrats'.

(3) Imagineers – leaders of the imagination whose institutional basis and visibility shifts and wanes. These may be in the public, private and voluntary sectors and in a wide variety of institutions and localities urban and rural.

It is the case that applying this framework to an individual city-region shows up a rich milieu of people interacting. However, at the pan-regional scale there are surprisingly few of them involved in motivating some of the new concepts. It views the interactions between the three as the key for an approach which focuses on the fine-grained effects of networks and partnerships within sub-national governance. The organisational consequences of the EU exit on the functioning of our profoundly centralised English state now come on top of this. Accepting that the current governing model is riven with structural inequalities, the starkest of which is found in the role of the geographies of prosperity and productivity I suggest that the 'slow crisis' of the governability of the country outside of the Greater South East region, has met the 'fast crisis' of a no-deal EU exit and that at their points of intersection currently sit highly combustible forces. Features of the fast include Strategic ambiguity and contrived randomness in EU exit. William Empson's 'constructive ambiguity' in governability.

There is a rich literature, mainly from within Industrial relations and political studies, about the question of the overall governability of contemporary societies. When couched in terms of animating governing capacity, institutional matrix or more conventionally the operating environment for subnational policy intervention, it posits that following the 'turn to governance' (market mechanisms lengthening the implementation supply chain of policy to include a broader implementation mix of public/private actors), the key question is about with whom the state might act in pursuit of its public policy objectives. These questions are particularly acute where weak and sub-ordinate sub-national governing authorities meet decisions about infrastructure spending. Sub-national and municipal authorities worldwide are in a process of continually reinventing themselves, with public transportation configured as both a function and a facilitator of governance scale, where right to exist, right to plan and ability to leverage resources combine. In Koiman's work on the system properties of governability he describes the interactive dynamic of systems working together. Infrastructure reconfigures the 'institutional matrix' of 'states' which have been hollowed in favour of 'the market' such that 'steering not rowing' is the most that government is able to do.

Meanwhile, within urban geography and economics the tradition expressed is that 'institutions matter' at the sub-national scale for growth, productivity and inclusion, and that appropriate sub-national scales must be strengthened. The two impulses lead to radically different policy prescriptions the former into an existential debate around the rights of institutions of government at every scale to govern. Analyses of local government, metropolitan and municipal government, the nations of the UK, who work the devolution settlements that they have agreed, despite the many asymmetries that these underpin. This has brought into even sharper relief as the sub-national policy space seeks to absorb the shock of Brexit – where the effects of economic restructuring will be felt most acutely in the period ahead.

This global and macrocontext swirling around the right to govern and with whom makes economic development interventions in the sub-national space and the construction of a weakly institutionalised scale of governance, such as the Northern Powerhouse, makes for a governing project of epic complexity. Furthermore, examination of the long traditions of regional planning and urban regime analysis appear to be absent from those advocating the current pan-northern scale, where a territory of 15 million people have governing requirements more akin to a small country. However, England lacks the formalised and constitutional structures of the devolved nations. Slow crisis therefore can be couched in terms of the wicked issues facing societies.

WICKEDNESS

Is the process one of re-scaling arenas from city and nation-state to 'urban region' and 'neighbourhood' with the consequent challenge to create a new territorial actor around a new arena and scale? Or is it the fragmentation there all the time for any analyst to see who looks carefully enough at the fine grain of urban governance processes ... should urban governance be understood as in continual transformation. (Healey, 2006)

It is clear that the network governance enthusiasts of the early twenty-first century such as Perri 6 and those anxious to frame public–private partnership in the modish language of as part of a 'relational' state, where connectivity within and between actors and agencies is the key (Mulgan, 2010). It argues that whether the jungles are green and leafy or concrete, they are brimming with intricate webs of relationships, which when viewed from afar, reveal elementary structures (Stephenson, 2004). The dark side of viewing networks as novel forms of governance was explained (Kooiman, 2003) in his book on networks. However, beyond some of the hyperbole there is a hope that the possibility of socially and spatially just outcomes could emerge from the mechanism mix as it is calibrated locally and in the specific junctures at which actors are able to exercise their preferred policy choices, the scope that they are able to exercise within their scale of operation (Haughton & Allmendinger, 2008). It explores what Kooiman (2003) calls the 'overall governability' of the North and argues that sub-national governance is underpowered in facing the challenges of uneven spatial development and the productivity and performance gaps between the regions of the United Kingdom. Healey (2006) attempts to reconcile these arguments by concentrating on the fragmentation, which is apparent from studying the fine-grain of institutional arrangements and dynamics. However, there can be a tendency in network analysis, for example, through ethnographic work on small-world research on the roles of street-level bureaucrats, to over emphasise the role of individuals at the expense of systems and structures.

The fine-grain then is viewed as necessary but not sufficient as these accounts must be tempered by advancing the understanding of the interpersonal chemistry of actor relationships within wider socio-political structures, as work on the relationship between partnership governance formations and the skill sets required to lead them successfully. The effects of governance formations on the individual agency of agents in networks, as brokers, and finding a place between policy entrepreneurs and pragmatic localists. Keith Grint has further developed this differentiation in his work on the social construction of leadership, arguing that leaders constitute and construct the social circumstances into which they are required to perform. This milieu, and context specificity is the key in framing the ability of leaders to lead. For Grint, the difference between management and leadership is the key, managers deal with the non-wicked issues and leaders are required for situations of genuine complexity. It follows, if you accept Grint's typology, that it is a leadership tactic to constitute reality in a dynamic way:

> *Dilemmas in a general theory of planning delimit the following list which is a far better way of exposing a truly wicked problem, unfortunately applying would make the cosy networked community governance model unworkable and consequently whilst wicked issues and complexity were rhetorically referred to local actors lacked the requisite power and autonomy to exercise their preferences.*
>
> *Their basic premise is that rational planning is unfit for the fluidity and discontinuity of the messiness of reality, and that a rational/ideal model is neither possible nor desirable.*

A great many barriers keep us from perfecting a planning and governing system that is adequate for decent forecasting, our intelligence is insufficient to our tasks, and the plurality of objectives held by the pluralities of politics:

> *make it impossible to pursue unitary aims ... the*
> *difficulties attached to rationality are tenacious and*
> *we have so far been unable to get untangled from*
> *their web.*
>
> *(Rittel & Webber, 1973, p. 160)*

This view, that a plurality of objectives held by plurality of politics make it impossible to pursue unitary aims chimes with Grint's belief in the increasing complexity of scenarios that require both collaborative resolution and is evident in Haughton and Allmendinger whose work on soft governance spaces points to the ways in which these are built and used. There are highly specific forms of metro political institution-building occurring at the interface between central and local policy-making. The implementation of public spending decisions specifically vis-á-vis the role of infrastructure is crucial. The close scholarship on the ways in which urban and rural elites engage in the reflexive process of making infrastructure decisions can be seen in the North's experience of collaborating through Transport for the North (TfN) or Northern Powerhouse Rail (NPR).

SCOPE AT SCALE FOR PLACE-BASED STATECRAFT

This heterodox analysis of the governability of the North of England can be found in urban and regional studies and at their point of intersection with organisational studies.

CONCLUSIONS: THE UNDERPOWERED NORTHERN POWERHOUSE AND THE UNGOVERNABLE NORTH

> *The guiding tenet in ... regime analysis (its 'iron*
> *law') is that for any governing arrangement to*

sustain itself, resources must be commensurate
with the agenda being pursued .... A companion
proposition is that for any substantial and sustained
agenda, a stable coalition is needed to provide the
necessary resources. (Stone, p. 103)

ARE CLARENCE STONE'S USA URBAN REGIMES FOR CITY REGIONS RELEVANT TO THE PAN-REGIONAL?

Urban regimes emerge from the concrete objectives and coalition building endeavours of resource-privileged actors. Stone's central point was that whatever the structural parameters, governing successfully depends on constructive political action to create durable alliances: regime building takes effort, and much of this effort is put into building the North's key city-regions, in Liverpool, Manchester, Sheffield, Leeds and Newcastle.

To analyse the Northern Powerhouse according to the iron law of regime analysis is to afford complicated and underpowered institutional paraphernalia the power of being a 'stable coalition'. The initiation rites of this proto-polity at the pan-northern scale are couched in terms of case-making for transformational infrastructure with the 'profound irrationalities' of mega-project development, described above by Easterling as Extra statecraft, and by Flyberg as governing projects where ...

[...] weakly institutionalised partnership space and a
brand-new institution at the northern scale (Transport
for the North) is supposed to 'go into governing
mode' and hop, skip and jump before it can walk.

This would be very hard to manage even in the context of the slow crisis of the English regions where the bleeding out of productivity and prosperity have only been accelerated following the 2008 banking crisis and the Austerian response of highly strategic state re-scaling. To add to this, the 'fast crisis' of EU exit, which, at the time of writing is profoundly unresolved, has ramifications far beyond the ambit of formal politics and has begun eating at the institutions of the British state one by one; this includes the judiciary, parliament and the civil service.

My thesis differentiates between the activities of these three cliques within the urban elite and the ways in which they discursively construct and maintain the brand of the city-regions. Elite interview data assembled at these local and city-regional scales are augmented by information derived from discussion with national decision-makers, to inform a wider account of the evolution of governance and policy-making. Based on my research I would argue that it is helpful to think of the Northern Powerhouse as follows in Table 1.1.

There can be no question that the Northern Powerhouse is a phenomenal brand. In consumer testing weighted for demographics it received 72% recognition with the general public. I have reflected more than once that each of those people has a very different view on what the Northern Powerhouse signifies!

Is then, the X factor for salience of a spatial scale to be found out with the formal institutions of government and bureaucracy? Is the lack of compelling imaginers of the northern powerhouse from the creative and cultural sectors a cause or an effect of the weakness of the sub-national institutional fix at the pan-regional scale?

Table 1.1. Northern Powerhouse and Its Stakeholders 2019.

	Brand	Plan	Strategy
Politicians and Bureaucrats	Northern Powerhouse branding, media campaign. 72% Recognition.	No national plan and no regional plans. Spatial consequences of policy not gathered at scale.	Industrial strategy and collection of LIS strategies insufficient at NPH scale.
Qualgaecrats Policy entrepreneurs Pragmatic localists	NPP highly visible as a lobbying group NP11 group of LEP chairs. RTPI and IPPR, RICS and others. Convention of the North.	One Powerhouse Great North Plan 2070 commission. All voluntarist or private spatial plans.	Partial strategies from TfN, the NPIER, Proposals from IPPR North, NPP the LIS processes, SIAs, NHSA and N8, the people's powerhouse.
Imagineers	Individual marketing efforts and products. Private Sector Corporates and Northern Entrepreneurs (e.g. Peel Holdings).	Not active at pan-regional scale. Often city-region focussed.	Not active at pan-regional scale.

Source: Headlam (2019).

What is the Northern Powerhouse Partnership?

The NPP will help develop consensus among businesses, civic leaders and others about how the north of England can be more successful. The focus will be on encouraging cities and counties to work together to create a northern powerhouse.

By producing original research, encouraging innovative thinking and hosting thought-provoking events, the NPP will encourage new policy ideas which will improve the north's quality of life and economy, and promote it as a place to work, study, live and invest.

The NPP is chaired by George Osborne and has a business-led Board which features influential business figures from across the North of England. Prominent city leaders across the region are also represented on the Board, in addition to Jim O'Neill, former Commercial Secretary to the Treasury, and John Cridland, Chair of Transport for the North (TfN). NPP is non-political and will maintain an all-party approach.

Note: The NPP, established by George Osborne, has a business-led board.

NOTE

1. This is a personal view after serving as a BEIS Industrial Strategy Fellow and Head of the Northern Powerhouse in 2018/19, and after conducting City-region research from 2010 onwards in Manchester and Liverpool. The chapter is based on a speech given in Newcastle upon Tyne at Northumbria University in March 2019.

2

COMBINED AUTHORITIES AND THE NORTHERN POWERHOUSE: CRITICAL ISSUES AND WHERE NEXT?

Joyce Liddle and John Shutt

INTRODUCTION

Our ongoing research is focussed on the changing framework for local and regional development in the UK and Europe, and we have a growing interest in leadership for city and regional development. The Organisation for Economic Co-operation and Development (OECD, 2009; 2010), in particular, has argued that city and regional leadership is now the key enabler of the growth of places.

Recently, Pugalis and Gray (2016) argued that 'Place-based Development' has replaced the 'old' paradigm of regional development with its focus on deprived and lagging regions to one based on institutional reform, multiactor collaboration, and with an underlying principle that all places have the potential for economic growth. Again, more recently, theory has centred on making sense of leadership in urban development.

The editors of this manuscript (Liddle & Shutt, 2019) have worked closely with Bentley, Pugalis and others over the past 10 years under the auspices of the Regional Studies Association to develop an international research network investigating 'Leadership in Urban and Regional Development' (Sotarauta, Beer, & Gibney, 2016).[1]

We organised a European Network examining leadership in different contexts, both Mayoral and Non-Mayoral across Europe, as well as investigating sub-national leadership in England, Australia, Finland, China and Europe. Our argument is that we need to make better sense of Place Leadership that is characterised by fragmented and shared actions; shared leadership across several organisations; multiscalar and dynamic interactive governance processes between many different actors, and should not simply accept 'top-down', informal processes which are imposed on regions from a Central State. Attention has focussed on the role of governance systems at the national scale in influencing the scope for leadership of development subnationally and in particular in examining highly centralised nations such as the UK, in contrast to federal systems like Germany.

A triadic concept of leadership, governance systems and central–local relations involves deliberative actions on how to influence different systems of government and what scope there is for place-based leadership (Bentley, Pugalis, & Shutt, 2017). They argue that the policy narrative of Local Enterprise Partnerships (LEPs) in England as localist vehicles, which in principle ought to engender strong leadership at sub-national scales, still is in fact a centralised system of government, with the effect that the LEPs are still subject to unyielding central controls and their hands are tied by funding deals and a shared national template of strategies. The danger is that we are embarking on a new UK Shared Prosperity Fund without any analysis of what has been achieved since 2010, under both the coalition and conservative governments. LEPs have received £9.1 billion of local growth funding since 2015–2016, with the northern regions 11 LEPs accounting for total funding of £3.4 billion (National Audit Office (NAO), 2019). There has been very little evaluation of the effectiveness of how this funding has been used to drive economic development and discussion of the relative merits of different strategies and programmes and priorities.

THE NEW AGE OF LEPS AND COMBINED AUTHORITIES AND A RENEWED PHASE OF NORTHERN POWERHOUSE DEVELOPMENT

We argue that, in the new age of the LEPs and the non-mayoral and Metro Mayoral Combined Authorities that have emerged, a new research agenda is needed to examine the scope for leadership at sub-national scales in different contexts. Moreover, we also point out that England is being fragmented by two different models of Combined Authorities and into which LEPs have now become submerged, and consequentially activities blurred.

Furthermore, since 2014, we have witnessed the rise of the new mega-level of 'regional concept': The Northern Powerhouse, the Midlands Engine and now the Oxford–Cambridge Corridor, which has thrown up a return to the pan- or mega-regional scale. It can be argued that this has been driven by central government, albeit supported by the Combined Authorities and LEPs and Mayors, but without a clear idea of leadership, detailed vision and clear focus on targets and desired outcomes. Clarity is required as to whether such initiatives fit in with the devolution process as a whole. The Central state appears happy to be seen to devolve transport, SME investment and Venture capital funds at this NP level, but it often feels like a top-down central state driven process rather than a bottom-up devolved one: it has again raised many issues about the future of the regional scale in England and explains why so many people despair at the ungovernability of the system which has been created. Many agencies have a partial view and there is insufficient consideration as to how the jigsaw fits together. This has been well explored in 2019 by Institute for Public Policy North (IPPR) North.

In Chapter 1, Dr Nicola Headlam reviews what the Northern Powerhouse achieved over the period 2014–2019 and sets the scene for a refreshing of the Northern Powerhouse Strategy. She seems to argue that the Northern Powerhouse is ungovernable as it stands. The strategy revision was underway already, but now we find suddenly in the summer of 2019 that the new Conservative leader and Prime Minister Boris Johnson has found a new Northern Powerhouse mojo. His government has now pledged renewed backing to the TfN Northern Powerhouse Rail project in Leeds and Manchester and this places the Prime Minister at the head of the New Towns Fund Programme, which aims to address some of the issues around the Key Cities and Towns programme. Moreover, the new PM confirmed his backing to Freeports, like the one proposed, and supported in Teesside by the Conservative Mayor, Ben Houchen.

So too has the Brexit Party, which now campaigns nationally for a new £200bn programme of Transport and Digital Infrastructure investment for regions outside London. These Conservative and Brexit parties continue the focus on Economic Growth issues in economic development and the Conservatives argue for the UK Shared Prosperity Fund to replace the existing European programmes, but as yet we have very little detail of what this new Fund might look like and what it might contribute to the North as a whole, let alone understand its impact across the three northern regions and across the new Combined Authorities, and across CORE and KEY cities.

In the North East there are now two Combined Authorities established, one for Tees Valley and one for the North of the Tyne. There is no coherent framework for the North East region as a whole and it could be argued that this framework is frustrating and fragmenting a serious debate on the future regional development. The North East LEP still operates at the level of the region as a whole but there is no real clarity at the moment on who speaks for the region and with regard to clarity of representation in the Northern Powerhouse operating structures, such as they exist. To add to the already confused governance picture, there is now a LEP Eleven board.[2] The chairs of each of the LEPs in the north of England sit on the newly formed government funded board and are called the 'NP11'. Operating inside the Northern Powerhouse, the six Combined Authority Mayors speak for their respective city-regions and organisations, like the IPPR North and Royal Town Planning Institute (RTPI), argue for still more effective bottom-up regional planning and a new plan for the North (Fig. 2.1).

POLICY TENSIONS AND THE PAST

Much of our own research work has focussed on trying to understand and make sense of both the institutional environment and the institutional arrangements of governance in England: often, as with devolution, with varying success.

Whereas in 1997 a certain level of optimism had returned and growth prospects began to improve: there was hope that

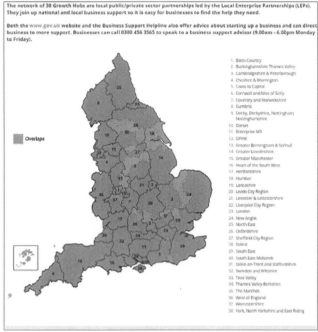

Fig. 2.1.   LEPs in England 2019.

Source: https://www.lepnetwork.net/growth-hubs/.

the UK state could be decentralised, not just with devolution, the new Regional Development Agencies (RDAs) and
a closer relationship to Europe, but in England, with the
Regional Assemblies as democratic regional governance.
However, the Assemblies failed to materialise. In the event
the RDAs themselves proved little more than a decade-long
experiment only to be abolished in what Vince Cable, the
then Business Minister, called the Coalition Government's
'Maoist moment'.

There have always been huge underlying policy tensions in the policy-making processes, as demonstrated by the Devolution plans under the Labour government that faltered with the North East Referendum on 4 November 2004, where voters rejected plans to establish an elected assembly for the regions. Three referendums were planned but only one took place and voters rejected the regional assembly proposals by 77.9–22.1% on a turnout of 48%. The defeat marked the end of the Labour government's policy for devolution and saw the cessations of plans for similar referendums in the North West and Yorkshire and the Humber regions.

The Cameron Coalition government period (in which the Conservatives took power/governed in collaboration with the Liberal Democrats) brought back a push for Localism and austerity and prioritised economic growth above all other priorities, but it did not dismantle the devolution settlement for Wales, Scotland and Northern Ireland. It did, however, strengthen the LEPs in 2014 by giving them responsibility for delivering the European Programmes for 2014–2020, thus maintaining multilevel governance and by giving joint responsibilities for Industrial Strategies at local levels. It also, from 2011 onwards, supported reforms of local government – the first since the metropolitan County Councils were abolished under the Thatcher government of 1996 – thereby allowing the formation of a set of City Region Combined Authorities, and encouraged the election of City Region Mayors, in places where there was popular support for them.

Much confusion still reigns as many have found it difficult to distinguish City Mayors from City Region Mayors (Hambleton & Sweeting, 2015) for an account of City Mayoral Governance, but not city regions. It is widely acknowledged that there is no coherent framework at the moment in England within which these devolution debates are proceeding (NAO, 2017) (see Fig. 2.2) and in a region like the North East

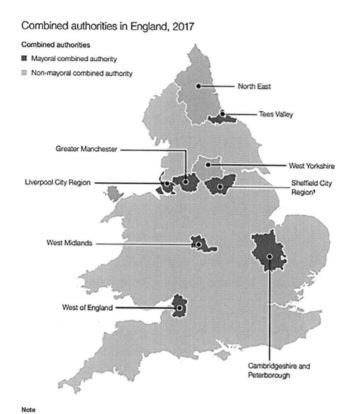

Combined authorities in England, 2017

Combined authorities

■ Mayoral combined authority

▨ Non-mayoral combined authority

Note

1   Sheffield City Region Combined Authority has a mayoral election planned for 2018.

Source: National Audit Office analysis of Office for National Statistics data

Fig. 2.2.   Combined Authorities in England, 2017.

Source: National Audit Office analysis of Office for NAO (2017).

one could argue that the level of current debate is too low and what little debate has taken place, remains the preserve of a few political elites.

LEPs, however, have been more absorbed into the new Combined Authorities. In total, nine Combined Authorities have been formed since 2011 and six (May 2017) have held their first Mayoral elections: Sheffield City Region is now the seventh, as from May 2018 and Cambridge and North of Tyne.

In the North East, the policy tensions were such that the idea for a proposed North East Combined Authority, covering the whole region, except the Tees Valley fell apart, to be replaced by a proposal to revive one Combined Authority only covering the territory of North of the Tyne (to include Newcastle upon Tyne, Northumberland and North Tyneside). North of Tyne Combined Authority only succeeded in electing its first Mayor in May 2019.

This North of Tyne CA leaves both parts of the North East and Yorkshire (16 local authorities support the new regional One Yorkshire proposal, but Sheffield and Rotherham local authorities do not) without an effective voice in the new Mayoral Combined Authority world which is emerging for the Northern Powerhouse. Fragmentation is the order of the day and there has been much discussion that Manchester is benefitting from the Northern Powerhouse to the exclusion of Yorkshire and the North East. Many argue that Manchester and Leeds are dominant across the Northern Powerhouse coverage/territory.

Commenting on the policy tensions, Lord John Prescott points out:

> *[...] we are still wrapped in that bit of Yorkshire independence that makes us want rows but not agreements ... We need to have a Yorkshire Plan. (Prescott, 2018)*

Headlam's argument is that the situation has become ungovernable and that rational Northern Powerhouse regional planning may be impossible in the current operating environment. Some hope not. The recent Kerslake UK 2070 Commission Report (Kerslake, 2019, May) and initiative argues for a revived budget for the Northern Powerhouse and the re-introduction of four new RDAs for England and a more serious approach to devolution in the forthcoming UK Spending review (Table 2.1 and Fig. 2.3).

Will these ideas gain any traction?

Successive governments have implemented policies to stimulate growth, swinging between local and regional level implementation, but it is also now becoming clearer that the pure economic growth model on its own is failing to deliver and a sustainable development and green model needs to predominate.

CONCLUSIONS: THE WIDENING NORTH–SOUTH DIVIDE

Alongside the fragmented devolution and Combined Authority arrangements, the North–South divide in the UK appears to be accelerating (Osborne, 2018), but there is also a new East–West divide (Hutton, 2018).There appears to be a withdrawal from evidence-based research and a confusion of regional and urban policy agendas, which McCann (2016) argues is producing:

> [...] a trajectory of a highly unbalanced governance system, with many decisions being made at the wrong spatial level ... and on many dimensions the UK is nowadays one of the world's most inter-regionally unbalanced and unequal economies and as a whole the UK economy is becoming increasingly de-coupled. (McCann, 2016)

Sub-national governments and Combined Authorities are an important part of challenging a strong centralised state and it is, perhaps, necessary to say that the time is right for a new round of localities research and capacity building, particularly once the BREXIT framework is known, looking at

Table 2.1.   The Local Election Results 2019: Local Authority Control in the North East Region.

Newcastle – Labour lost two council seats and saw its share of the vote drop 10%, as community party Newcastle First made history by winning its first election Newcastle upon Tyne: LD gain 1, Ind gain 1, Lab lose 2. New council: Lab 54, LD 20, Ind 4.

Gateshead – The Lib Dems snatched two seats from Labour councillors, but Labour still retain control of the authority Gateshead: LD gain 2, Lab lose 2. New council: Lab 52, LD 14.

North Tyneside – Labour remains comfortably in control despite losing two seats – Cullercoats and Tynemouth – to the Tories North Tyneside: C gain 1, Lab lose 1. New council: Lab 51, C 7, Ind 1, LD 1.

North Tyneside: C gain 1, Lab lose 1. New council: Lab 51, C 7, Ind 1, LD 1 South Tyneside – Labour have taken a bruising after losing five seats, four to independent candidates and one to the council's first ever Green Party councillor.

Sunderland – A 'free for all' at the polls saw Labour lose 10 seats, while breakthroughs by the Greens and UKIP saw both parties enter the chamber for the first time.

Cons gain 4, UKIP gain 3, LD gain 2, Green gain 1, Lab lose 9, Ind lose 1. New council: Lab 51, C 12, LD 8, UKIP 3, Green 1.

Hartlepool: Lab lose to no overall control. Ind gain 3, UKIP gain 1, Lab lose 4. New council: Ind 16, Lab 13, C 3, UKIP 1 Darlington: Lab lose to NOC. C gain 7.

Stockton-on-Tees: Lose to NOC Ind gain 3, C gain 2, LD gain 1, Lab lose 6. New council: Lab 24, Ind 16, C 14, LD 2 Middlesbrough: Lab lose to NOC. Ind.

Middlesbrough: Lab lose to NOC. Ind gain 13, Lab lose 11, C lose 2. New council: Ind 23, Lab 20.

Mayoral Elections 2019: Middlesborough Council-Ind Mayor win
Andy Preston (Ind) 17,418 (59.18%, +0.69%).

Mick Thompson (Lab) 6,693 (22.74%, −11.00%).

Peter Longstaff (Ind) 2,940 (9.99%).

Ken Hall (C) 2,382 (8.09%, +0.32%).

Electorate 94,710; Turnout 29,433 (31.08%, −19.85%).

North of Tyne Combined Authority – Labour win.

*Jamie Driscoll (Lab) 62,034 (33.91%).

Charlie Hoult (C) 45,494 (24.87%).

John McCabe (Ind) 31,507 (17.22%).

John Appleby (LD) 23,768 (12.99%).

William Hugh Jackson (UKIP) 20,131 (11.00%).

Eliminated: John Appleby, William Hugh Jackson and John McCabe.

(Second Count): Distribution of Appleby's, Jackson's and McCabe's votes.

Jamie Driscoll (Lab) 76,862.

Charlie Hoult (C) 60,089.

* which denotes first count in brackets to correspond with later second count

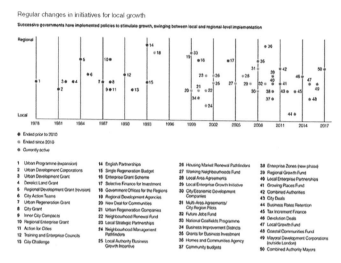

Regular changes in initiatives for local growth

Successive governments have implemented policies to stimulate growth, swinging between local and regional-level implementation

● Ended prior to 2010
◐ Ended since 2010
○ Currently active

1 Urban Programme (expansion)	14 English Partnerships	26 Housing Market Renewal Pathfinders	38 Enterprise Zones (new phase)
2 Urban Development Corporations	15 Single Regeneration Budget	27 Working Neighbourhoods Fund	39 Regional Growth Fund
3 Urban Development Grant	16 Enterprise Grant Scheme	28 Local Area Agreements	40 Local Enterprise Partnerships
4 Derelict Land Grant	17 Selective Finance for Investment	29 Local Enterprise Growth Initiative	41 Growing Places Fund
5 Regional Development Grant (revision)	18 Government Offices for the Regions	30 City/Economic Development Companies	42 Combined Authorities
6 City Action Teams	19 Regional Development Agencies		43 City Deals
7 Urban Regeneration Grant	20 New Deal for Communities	31 Multi-Area Agreements/City Region Pilots	44 Business Rates Retention
8 City Grant	21 Urban Regeneration Companies	32 Future Jobs Fund	45 Tax Increment Finance
9 Inner City Compacts	22 Neighbourhood Renewal Fund	33 National Coalfields Programme	46 Devolution Deals
10 Regional Enterprise Grant	23 Local Strategic Partnerships	34 Business Improvement Districts	47 Local Growth Fund
11 Action for Cities	24 Neighbourhood Management Pathfinders	35 Grants for Business Investment	48 Coastal Communities Fund
12 Training and Enterprise Councils		36 Homes and Communities Agency	49 Mayoral Development Corporations (outside London)
13 City Challenge	25 Local Authority Business Growth Incentive	37 Community budgets	50 Combined Authority Mayors

Fig. 2.3.   Regular Changes in Initiatives for Growth.

Source: NAO (2017).

the local economy futures of both city and county areas and increasing the role of the new Combined Authorities in economic and social development in the decade ahead.

A new Northern Powerhouse Convention and Regional Assembly would help rather than hinder in the current Brexit moment and would focus on new post-2020 demands. We need to take a fresh look at:

- The insights into changing work and employment policies and their impact on labour markets and local economies across the Northern Powerhouse.

- The focus on practitioners and the ability to help them engage with the multiscalar policy process in a variety of contexts across the north of England and to assist them to engage nationally and with the European Union and at the global scale.

- The ability to make sense of the complex multilevel governance arrangements and to bring together institutional frameworks in regional governance in a way in which helps clarify theories, methods, policy and politics is becoming more crucial especially as regional coalitions are multiplying.

- Making use of institutional changes to develop place leadership, exploring new ways of examining local economy and city–region and regional governance changes and examining the policy tensions and paradoxes of policy development under different political regimes which are often fast-changing.

- The ability to use international comparisons and examine the implications of the policy transfer process at a global level.

- The focus on locality research, regional research, urban management practice as well as urban regeneration and place management and leadership as a distinct activity.

NOTES

1. See also www.placeleadershipnetwork.org.

2. LEP 11 Board was formed in 2018 and includes all eleven (11) LEP Northern Chairs.

3

THE NHS LONG-TERM PLAN AND THE IMPORTANCE TO THE NORTH EAST REGION

Debbie Porteous

INTRODUCTION

The Long-term Plan (LTP) for the National Health Service (NHS, 2019) identifies a blueprint to make the NHS fit for the future with a greater focus on prevention, improving services for patients and the importance of integrating services to make them more effective and efficient. The challenge is in the delivery and who is responsible to implement. The key is to enable staff at local level to have responsibility to ensure the health and social needs of their local population are met. To support local planning, local health systems will receive five year indicative financial allocations for 2019–2024 and be asked to produce local plans for implementation. Established to guide the implementation is a National Health Service Assembly who advise the joint boards of NHS England and NHS Improvement on delivery of the

NHS LTP. This requires shared commitment and motivation to change; ensuring patient centred care is at the forefront of any changes to delivering care. At regional level, Sustainability and Transformation Partnerships (STPs)[1] and Integrated Care Systems (ICSs)[2] are groups of local NHS organisations, local councils and other partners who are working together in the region to develop and implement the plan. There are many challenges ahead to ensure the plan delivers regional health and social care, including the United Kingdom's decision to leave the European Union. This chapter will focus on the implications of the LTP for the North East of England. In addition, Brexit has major implications for health and social care in the UK. These have recently been explored by the King's Fund. Brexit has already had an impact on the retention of EU nationals, which is contributing to staff shortages in the NHS (NHS, 2019e).

It is well-documented (Jagger, 2015; NHS, 2014, *Five Year Forward View*) that the NHS has experienced an increase in demand for services over the past decade which has led to an increase in costs of delivering those services. Cuts to public health and social care funding have added further pressure. As a result, the NHS and social care continue to face many challenges that include workforce shortages and key performance targets not met.

In June 2018, the Prime Minister announced a new five-year funding settlement for the NHS: a 3.4% average real-terms annual increase in NHS England's budget between 2019/20 and 2023/24 (a £20.5 billion increase over the period). To unlock this funding, national NHS bodies were asked to develop a LTP for the service. The resulting document, the NHS LTP, was published on 7 January 2019 (NHS, 2019). The plan builds on the policy platform laid out in the *NHS Five Year Forward View* (NHS, 2014) which articulated the need to integrate care to meet the needs of a changing population. This was followed by subsidiary strategies, covering General Practice (GP), cancer, mental health and maternity services, while the new models of care outlined in the Forward View have been rolled out through a programme of vanguard[3] sites NHS England (2016).

It is important to note that the LTP applies to the NHS only and not to the whole health and care system. The plan clearly identifies that to progress it will rely on action from social care and public health, as it is only one part of the jigsaw. If implemented as proposed it will set the direction of the NHS by focussing on delivering joined-up, personalised, preventive care and expanding primary and community services.

FOCUS ON HEALTH CARE IN THE NORTH EAST

The North East has strong acute and primary health services and increases in life expectancy along with reductions in smoking have been greater than elsewhere in the UK (Public Health England, 2019b). Although it is recognised that health inequalities within the region continue to exist[4] and on average, people living in the most deprived local authorities in the North East have a life expectancy of around six months shorter than those in the rest of England (Bambra et al., 2018). To improve the lives of people in the North East you cannot view health needs in isolation. There is a requirement for local government to focus on effective public policies that address economic, social and environmental policies. The focus requires being on prevention and improving outcomes across the life cycle that includes schooling readiness, good and fulfilling employment to healthy and independent old age (North East Combined Authority (NECA), 2016).

Health services in the North East region serve a varied geographical area. The area represents around two million people, which includes urban centres and inner city areas, suburbs and commuter villages, and significant rural areas in the north and west comprising market towns, villages and some of the most sparsely populated areas of England.

SO WHAT ARE THE IMPLICATIONS OF THE LTP FOR THE HEALTH NEEDS OF THE LOCAL POPULATION?

The focus on prevention and improving outcome is a step in the right direction. The overarching strategic direction of the plan is to continue to build on the foundations of the *NHS Five Year Forward View* (NHS, 2014) by ensuring everyone gets the best start in life, delivering excellent care for major health problems and supporting people to age well. In effect, a new service model for the twenty-first century. Five significant changes are outlined to the NHS service model; greater integration of primary and community health services, redesign and reduced pressure on emergency hospital services, people will have more control over their own health with personalised care packages, a focus on population health with an emphasis on local partnerships with local authority-funded services, and digitally enabled primary and outpatient care.

CLINICAL PRIORITIES

There is a clear focus on measurable improvements in health outcomes. These priorities include cancer, cardiovascular disease (CVD), maternity and neonatal health, mental health, stroke, diabetes and respiratory care. There is also a strong focus on children and young people's health. The plan also sets out a number of actions to improve detection and care for people with CVD and respiratory disease, prevent diabetes and improve stroke services. The aim is to prevent up to 150,000 cases of heart attack, stroke and dementia over the next 10 years. Trends in diabetes, overweight and excess alcohol consumption are increasing in the North East and the region currently ranks among the highest on diabetes, CVD, stroke, excess alcohol consumption and obesity as well as mental ill health in women (Public Health England, 2015). These commitments to improve health outcomes will save lives but requires clear national and local leadership, an increase in current workforce capacity and investment in diagnostic equipment. In addition, to be considered is the growing need of individuals with multiple complex needs.

PRIMARY AND COMMUNITY SERVICES

Improving care outside hospitals is one of the headline commitments in the plan. It clearly identifies by 2023/24, funding for primary and community care will be at least £4.5 billion higher than in 2019/20. The plan confirms that GPs will join to form primary care networks. Groups of neighbouring practices typically covering 30–50,000 people. GP will enter network contracts, alongside their existing contracts, which will include a single fund through which network resources will flow.

Primary care networks will be expected to take a proactive approach to managing population health and from 2020/21 will assess the needs of their local population to identify people who would benefit from targeted, proactive support. Improving local public health in the North East by investing in prevention is welcome. Alongside primary care networks, the plan commits to developing 'fully integrated community-based health care'. This will involve developing multidisciplinary teams, including GPs, pharmacists, district nurses and allied health professionals working across primary care and hospital sites. Over the next five years, all parts of the country will be required to increase capacity in these teams so that crisis response services can meet response times set out in guidelines by the National Institute for Health and Care Excellence (2018). Collaboration in primary care takes time and requires a shared vision, strong relationships and effective leadership.

MENTAL HEALTH AND LEARNING DISABILITIES

In adult services the aim is to create a more comprehensive service with a single point of access for adults and children and 24/7 support with appropriate responses across NHS. There are two significant commitments to developing new models of care. The first is to create a comprehensive offer for children and young people, from birth to age 25, with a view to tackling problems with transitions of care. The second is to redesign core community mental health services by 2023/24, reinforcing components such as psychological therapies, physical health care and employment support, as well as introducing personalised care and restoring substance misuse support within NHS mental health services. These commitments will include new waiting time standards covering emergency mental health services by 2020, children and young people's mental health services and, over the next decade, adult community mental health treatment.

To support these changes, the plan mandates that investment in children and young people's mental health provision will grow faster than the overall NHS budget and total mental health spending. Within the North East, children and adults have similar levels of wellbeing to the rest of the country in part due to good health services, high levels of social cohesion and green environments with relatively low air pollution, which support mental health (Public Health England, 2019). However, there are challenges unique to the North East. The mental health of pregnant women and new mothers identifies 10–20% experiencing mental health problems. Poor maternal or paternal mental health will give children the unhealthiest start in life. The region also has very high numbers of vulnerable children; 92 in every 10,000 children in the region are in care; 31 in every 10,000 are in care as a result of neglect or abuse; a quarter of all children in the North East live in poverty; and an estimated 10% young people must be a focus for support if we are to improve their life chances. Among adults, we have higher levels of mental health problems in the region, more substance misuse (particularly alcohol) and high levels of self-harm (Public Health England, 2019).

EMERGENCY HOSPITAL SERVICES

The plan builds on previous initiatives, which include clinical streaming on entering Accident and Emergency (A&E) and same day emergency care (also known as ambulatory emergency care). This will see some patients admitted from A&E undergo diagnosis and treatment in quick succession so that they can be discharged on the same day, rather than staying in hospital overnight. Urgent treatment centres will increase and will be GP-led facilities that include access to diagnostics and offer appointments bookable via NHS 111[5] for patients who do not need the expertise available at A&E departments. Alongside this, the plan aims to improve the advice available to patients over the phone and extend support for staff in the community by introducing a multidisciplinary clinical assessment service as part of the NHS 111 service in 2019/20.

DIGITAL

Digital technology is a key feature in the plan, with ambitious patient-facing targets identified. The NHS app[6] will act as a gateway for people to access services and information; by 2020/21, people will be able to use it to access their care plan and communications from health professionals. From 2024, patients will have a new 'right' to access digital primary care services (e.g. online consultations), either via their existing practice or one of the emerging digital-first providers. By the end of the 10-year period covered by the plan, the vision is for people to be increasingly cared for and supported at home using remote monitoring (via wearable devices) and digital tools. To deliver 'digitally enabled care' all secondary care providers become 'fully digitised' by 2024. This will involve NHS organisations putting in place electronic records and a range of other digital capabilities. The Global Digital Exemplars programme (NHS, 2019a) will create models for technology adoption and a shared record through Local Health and Care Record. An example is the Great North Care Record.[7] To facilitate these changes NHS organisations will be required to have a chief clinical information officer or chief information officer at board level by 2021/22. Similarly, to promote interoperability, there is now a commitment to introduce controls to ensure that technology suppliers to the NHS comply with agreed standards (Gov.UK, 2016, 2018a). To implement funding requires to be secured and recognition of the digital infrastructure to support, such as mobile internet connectivity needs to be clearly outlined. Consideration of the workforce and patients alike need to be supported to use digital tools and understand and act on the data they generate (NHS England, 2019b. *The Topol review*).

FROM PLANNING TO DELIVERY AT LOCAL LEVEL

The LTP marks a significant step forward in setting the NHS on a sustainable course for the next decade. It is clearly focussed on delivering joined-up, personalised, preventive care and expanding primary and community services. The main challenge will be to translate this into delivery. Leadership, funding, workforce requirements are pivotal in delivering. To achieve implementation, the approach to delivering the plan balances national direction with local autonomy. National expectations are made clear and local systems will be accountable for contributing to national programmes. The plan implies clinicians and leaders who are directly accountable for patient care will lead that local implementation. The Interim NHS People Plan (NHS, 2019c) developed collaboratively with national leaders and partners sets a vision for how people working in the NHS will be supported to deliver care and identifies the actions required at national, regional, ICSs and local organisations (trusts, clinical commissioning groups and primary care networks). This means that local systems are central to the delivery of the plan.

Dame Jackie Daniel, Chief Executive of The Newcastle upon Tyne Hospitals NHS Foundation Trust is one of the 50 individuals from across the health and care sector appointed to the NHS Assembly (NHS, 2019d)[8] to advise the NHS England and NHS Improvement Joint Board at regular intervals on the implementation of the improvements it outlined.

Dame Jackie Daniel identifies that for the region:

> *The NHS Long Term Plan creates significant opportunities for the work underway in the North East and North Cumbria. It supports many of our priorities over the next five years. These include:*

- *Clinical Priorities* – the plan proposes a range of clinical priorities. These include children and young people, cancer, CVD, stroke, respiratory disease and mental health. These are all important areas for improvement across our region.

- *Primary and Community Services, Integrated Care and Population Health* – as an ICS we will work on an earned autonomy basis and support place based population health. The £4.5 billion uplift to primary medical and community health services will provide a much-needed boost to out of hospital services.

- *Workforce* – although a key risk, it is anticipated that the detail on staffing will come alongside the People Plan (NHS 2019c) supported by a new national workforce group.

- *Digital* – a major focus of work to transform care. The 'Great North Care Record'[9] – will support patient experience. A potential game changer for the population and future generations.

> *A region with a good track record and high ambition – but with poor health outcomes. We welcome the focus on prevention and health inequalities.*

The plan clearly focusses on health inequalities making it a key priority. The commitment to establishing specific goals for reducing inequalities in the North East is particularly welcome. The plan signals a clear focus on prevention, recognising that the NHS can take important action to complement the role of local authorities and the contribution of government, communities, industry and individuals. A 'renewed' NHS prevention programme will focus on maximising the role of the NHS in influencing behaviour change. This is guided by the top five risk factors identified by the Global Burden of Disease Study (Steel et al., 2018) which are smoking, poor diet, high blood pressure, obesity and alcohol and drug use.

The success of smoking cessation work in the North East demonstrates what can be achieved. Around 15 people in the North East die each day from smoking, and smoking is estimated to cost society approximately £775m each year in the North East. For these reasons the North East has been at the forefront of tackling smoking levels via the Fresh North East programme.[10] Across the region Fresh has contributed to smoking declining by more than a third from 2005 to 2015, the biggest decline of any region in England and smoking-related mortality declining faster than the national average. In addition, the BabyClear[11] programme to reduce smoking rates in pregnancy has seen maternal smoking rates fall by 4% since implementation compared to 2.6% nationally (Bell, Glinianaia, & Waal, 2018). If this work was replicated across the whole of the NHS, social care, community and voluntary sector organisations there would be a measurable change in smoking reduction.

The planning process required local teams to consider how to adapt existing programmes to better address health inequalities. One of those existing programmes commissioned for the north is The Equality and Health Inequalities Right Care Pack[12] that considers measures of health inequality and aims to support health systems to identify areas of improvement in promoting equality and reducing health inequalities within local areas (NHS, 2018a). This renewed approach is underpinned by additional funding channelled to the poorest parts of the country worth over £1 billion a year over and above what they would ordinarily have received by 2023/24. These data can be accessed in the Right Care pack for the North[13] (NHS, 2018b). The NHS cannot treat people out of inequality but the gap can be closed if there is focussed partnership working with local councils, the voluntary sector and communities themselves.

ICSs are identified as key in addressing improvements in population health and tackle the wider determinants of ill health. The NHS Confederation recently published *Defining the role of Integrated Care Systems (ICSs) in workforce development: a draft manifesto* (NHS Confederation, 2019a) identified that ICSs are accountable for system wide workforce decision-making. However, their development is currently much more advanced in some areas than others are, and even the most advanced systems are in their early stages. ICSs have no formal powers or accountabilities and progress is dependent on the willingness of individuals and strength of local relationships. There are also high expectations on primary care networks as the key mechanism for delivering the expansion in primary and community services outlined in the plan. However, they are a long way from existing in the form or on the scale envisaged. Providing support for ICSs and primary care networks and building local leadership capacity and capability should therefore be key priorities. National bodies are required to support local implementation and remove barriers, within existing legislation.

Workforce shortage remains a key risk to delivery. The health and social care sectors have relied on EU and other foreign nationals in all parts of the workforce and will continue to need them in the future. The unknown uncertainties related to the Brexit impact on recruitment. The EU settlement scheme (Gov.UK, 2018b) concerning the status of EU citizens currently living in the UK will provide some reassurance for current staff to stay and continue to make a valuable contribution to the health and social care workforce. The plan identifies a number of specific measures to address national recruitment targets. However, many wider changes will not be finalised until after the 2019 Major Spending Review (now delayed until after the expected British General Election in 2019 and expected in 2020), when the budget for training, education and continuing professional development is set. To inform these reforms, NHS Improvement, Health

Education England and NHS England will establish a cross-sector national workforce group and publish a workforce implementation plan later in 2019. An interim plan has been published (NHS, 2019c) which gives insight into proposed actions to address workforce issues.

In the longer term, while efforts are welcomed to increase the domestic NHS workforce, it will take time for many of these policies to result in extra staff on the front line. Providers of NHS and social care services need the ability to recruit staff from the EU and other countries when there are not enough resident workers to fill vacancies.

Consideration for workforce planning also needs to include thinking through how the NHS can work much more effectively with partners outside the health service. Good health depends not just on the NHS but also on the social care system; and an effective training pipeline of skilled staff requires strong partnership with further education institutions and universities, especially if opportunities are broadened to ensure that the NHS has a diverse staff group that reflects the society it serves. The role of education institutions and universities is not transparent in the plan and there are a number of actions required to further integrate health and social care. An example of recent success within the North East is the National Institute for Health Research has announced it's funding for Applied Research Collaborations[14] to tackle key issues facing our health and social care system, including increasing demands on services due to an ageing population and aspects linked to austerity. A new government £16 million health improvement programme[15] in the North East and North Cumbria has been awarded to a collaboration led by Newcastle University and hosted by Northumberland, Tyne and Wear NHS Foundation Trust. Themes will focus on aspects such as prevention of poor health, staying healthy with long-term conditions, supporting children and families, integrating health and social care for physical and mental health difficulties, inequalities across communities, using new technology and information to improve lives.

To address inequalities in health and secure and sustain the economic and social health wellbeing of people the recommendations of the LTP will build upon current research which includes implementation of the recommendations of Due North report (Public Health England, 2015), the Health for Wealth report (Bambra et al., 2018) and Well North (2019) to form the Northern Universities' Public Health Alliance (NUPHA)[16] working with the Northern Health Science Alliance[17] and N8 Research partnership.[18]

CONCLUSION

The NHS LTP is forward-thinking and there is a clear commitment to improving prevention and reducing health inequalities, which will be of significant benefit to the North east. The plan includes a commitment to increasing support for people to manage their own health and highlights the need to create genuine partnerships between professionals and patients. This has the potential to make a significant difference to patients and change how they interact with health services. Potential benefits include: more NHS support for people in care homes; better access to services spanning mental health, GP and community crisis response teams; fewer trips to outpatient appointments; more services and information available online; and more opportunities for people to make decisions about their own care. The key to success is working with the sector to ensure resources follow the patient and that the wide variety of advice, social activities and voluntary sector support on which social prescribing is based, can continue to respond to the ever increasing demand and increase in referrals from GPs and other clinicians.

Its limitations are that a plan for the NHS cannot be achieved by the NHS in isolation. Partnerships between the NHS and local government will be key to delivering improvements in population health. To deliver high quality care leadership is key. To build these capabilities, there is a requirement to support leaders, including development of cultural values and beliefs of compassion, inclusion and collaboration across the NHS (Fig. 3.1).

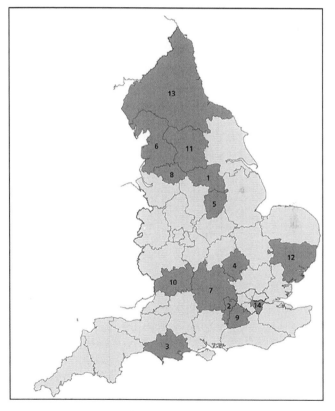

Fig. 3.1.   Map of Integrated Care Systems.

Source: National Health Service England (2019e).

In 2016, NHS organisations and local councils came together to form 44 STPs covering the whole of England, and set out their proposals to improve health and care for patients.

The North East and North Cumbria (13) has become the country's largest ICS, serving more than three million people alone. The link between the NHS regional Plan, monitoring the impact of Brexit on the NHS and the announcements made in October 2019 of an expansion of NHS expenditures by the Boris Johnson Conservative government all remain critical to the health economy and future of the North East region and their implications remain to be understood.

THE NHS PLAN IN THE NORTH EAST REGION

Dame Jackie Daniel Chief Executive of Newcastle upon Tyne Hospitals NHS Foundation Trust is one of the 50 individuals from across the health and care sector appointed to the NHS Assembly (NHS, 2019d) to advise the NHS England and NHS Improvement at regular intervals on the implementation of the improvements it outlined.

ACKNOWLEDGEMENTS

The author thanks Dame Jackie Daniel, Chief Executive of Newcastle upon Tyne Hospitals NHS Foundation Trust.

NOTES

1. In 2016 the NHS and local councils came together in 44 areas covering all of England to develop proposals to improve health

and care. They formed new partnerships known as STPs: https://www.england.nhs.uk/integratedcare/stps/.

2. ICSs are local partnerships to improve health and care: https://www.england.nhs.uk/integratedcare/.

3. There are five vanguard models which can be viewed www.england.nhs.uk/vanguards.

4. See map at https://fingertips.phe.org.uk/profile/public-health-outcomes-framework/data#page/8/gid/1000049/pat/6/par/E12000001/ati/101/are/E06000057.

5. NHS 111 allows patients to get urgent healthcare online or via telephone: https://www.england.nhs.uk/urgent-emergency-care/nhs-111/.

6. NHS app simple and secure way to access a range of NHS services on your smartphone or tablet: https://www.nhs.uk/using-the-nhs/nhs-services/the-nhs-app/.

7. Great North Care Record. Is an electronic platform that enables sharing of patient information within the region: https://www.greatnorthcarerecord.org.uk/.

8. The NHS Assembly will bring together a range of individuals from across the health and care sectors at regular intervals to advise the joint boards of NHS England and NHS Improvement on delivery of the NHS Long Term Plan (LTP): https://www.longtermplan.nhs.uk/nhs-assembly/.

9. Great North Care record. Is an electronic platform that enables sharing of patient information within the region: https://www.greatnorthcarerecord.org.uk/.

10. Fresh was the UK's first dedicated regional programme set up in the North East in 2005 to tackle the worst rates of smoking related illness and death in England: http://www.freshne.com/.

11. An evidence-based stop-smoking intervention called 'BabyClear' increased the chance that pregnant smokers in North East England managed to 'quit' smoking by the time of delivery: https://discover.dc.nihr.ac.uk/content/signal-000403/the-babyclear-programme-helped-pregnant-women-stop-smoking-in-north-east-england.

12. Equality and Health Inequality NHS Right Care Packs. They aim to support health and care systems design and deliver services that work to reduce health inequalities in access to services and health outcomes for their diverse local populations: https://www.en gland.nhs.uk/rightcare/products/ccg-data-packs/equality-and-health-inequality-nhs-rightcare-packs/.

13. The Equality and Health Inequalities Right Care Pack North considers measures of health inequality and aims to support CCGs and health systems to identify areas of improvement in promoting equality and reducing health inequalities: https://www.england.nhs.uk/publication/equality-and-health-inequalities-packs-2018-north/.

14. NIHR: https://www.nihr.ac.uk/explore-nihr/support/collaborating-in-applied-health-research.htm.

15. Multimillion pound investment to improve the region's health: https://www.ncl.ac.uk/press/articles/latest/2019/07/appliedresearchcollaboration/.

16. Northern Universities' Public Health Alliance: https://www.ncl.ac.uk/press/articles/latest/2019/07/nupha/.

17. Northern Health Science Alliance: http://www.thenhsa.co.uk/.

18. The N8 Research Partnership's main research areas have been chosen based on existing research strengths in the N8 universities and the potential for growth and economic impact: https://www.n8research.org.uk/.

PART II

THE IMPACTS OF BREXIT AND KEY POLICY AREAS

4

DEVELOPING A POST-BREXIT ECONOMY: CHALLENGES FOR THE NORTH EAST OF ENGLAND

Ignazio Cabras

INTRODUCTION

Since the triggering of Article 50, the uncertainty around Brexit and the outcomes of the UK/EU negotiations process associated with the UK leaving the EU have catalysed the British political debate. This situation has had and still has significant economic implications for thousands of businesses operating in the UK. Nevertheless, it is likely that impact of Brexit will be much larger for the North East of England (NE) compared to other English regions, despite the Leave vote winning an overwhelming majority in the region. In fact, many areas in the NE have relied heavily on public sector jobs and investments in the past and benefited from substantial European funding provided over the last few decades to support infrastructure, regeneration and training activities. Over 70,000 jobs were created in the area as a result of EU investments between 2007 and 2013, and thousands of jobs still depend on investments made in the 2014–2020 period. There is a widespread concern, particularly among small businesses, regarding levels of inward investments post-Brexit. Moreover, there are clear threats to sectors that depend on exports to other EU countries. This will include production units that are part of large multinationals that export high value manufacturing and processing activities such as vehicles, electronics and pharmaceuticals. This chapter will address and analyse the economic implications that Brexit could generate for the NE. Focussing on data gathered from various sources in the aftermath of the referendum, the author examines the most recent findings in literature in view of critically evaluating and assessing what a post-Brexit NE may be like from an economic and social perspective.

THE BREXIT VOTE IN THE NORTH EAST

The Leave campaign registered an impressive result in the NE: only one constituency out of 12 across the region voted to remain, with a leave vote of over 60% in half of the constituencies. This is despite the NE benefiting heavily from EU structural fund investments and experiencing comparatively low numbers of migrant workers relative to other English regions. However, while the EU funds brought significant improvements in the infrastructural endowments, and investments linked with EU sources accounting for an estimated 141,000 jobs in the region, the difference between the NE and other regions has increased in the past two decades (Cabras et al., 2018). Fig. 4.1 shows the gross disposable household income (GDHI) by UK regions at 2016 price basis (ONS, 2016). The NE is the second lowest figure among all regions considered, with only Northern

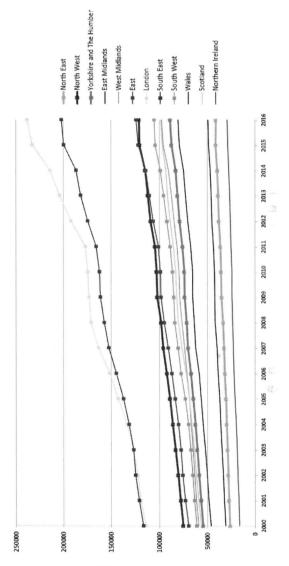

Fig. 4.1. Regional GDHI at Current Basic Prices.

Ireland performing worse in the 16-year period analysed. Among English regions, the NE saw the slowest growth rate between 1997 and 2016, and although the NE average income per head grew £9.2–15.3K during the period considered, it is now more than three times lower than the average income per head in inner London (£48K). Marked interregional inequalities had an impact in the voting intention of many in the regions, as indicated by McCann (2019, forthcoming) in his recent study of the economies of discontent.

In such a context, the implication of any outcome generated by the Brexit process are significant for the NE and the UK overall, given the considerable exposure of businesses, supply chains and jobs in terms of commercial exchanges. In 2014, the EU was the UK's main trading partner, taking 45% of UK exports and providing 53% of the UK's imports of goods and services. At the same time, EU countries accounted for £453bn, the largest source of inward investment in the UK worth 46% of the total inward FDI (Cabras et al., 2018).

Estimates released by the UK government in January 2018, nearly one and a half years following the referendum, predicted a 15-year impact on the UK economy of three main scenarios: staying in the single market, doing a trade deal with the EU or leaving with no deal. Findings from the report identified sectors such as chemicals, food and drink, clothes, manufacturing, automotive and retail as the most affected given their relative share of trade with the EU and the trade intensity of their inputs. Projected Gross Value Added (GVA) in these sectors would decrease by between 2% and 8% depending on the negotiated trade agreement at a UK level from 2019 until 2034. New trade deals signed with third party countries and regulatory opportunities that might emerge from an agreed UK/ EU deal would not be able to offset some of the effects of lost markets on these sectors. In addition, according to the report, there would be significant variation in terms of how the Brexit process would affect different areas and regions in the country, although it suggests that the NE and West Midlands would see the biggest impact to growth. In the worst case scenario, a 'no deal' Brexit that would reverse UK/EU exchanges to World Trade Organisation rules, the NE would face a potential decrease of 16% of GVA.

A study published by Chen et al. (2018) examined the exposure of UK and EU Nomenclature of Territorial Units for Statistics (NUTS) 2 level regions to Brexit. Focussing on trade linkages across regions and addressing scale and nature of exchanges between the UK and the EU, the authors developed an index encompassing production processes within 245 regions across the 28 EU member states, using data from the World Input–Output Database. In particular, the index investigated economic risks and issues associated with the size and relevance of trade and commerce associated with productive processes, assessing the potential economic shock for regions and countries in case of a 'no deal' scenario between the UK and EU.

According to Chen et al. (2018) and analysing gross domestic product (GDP) and labour income at a regional level, UK regions result significantly more exposed to Brexit than other EU regions, except for Irish regions which face a similar level of exposure. The authors suggest that many of the UK's least powerful regions are the ones more affected by the Brexit process and any associated outcomes: UK regions result an average of 4.6 times more exposed compared to all the remaining EU regions, with a large number of EU regions facing almost no exposure at all. Moreover, the authors predict about 2.6% of EU GDP at risk because of Brexit trade related consequences, whereas this risk is estimated at 12.2% for UK GDP – about six times higher.

Table 4.1 shows results extracted from Chen et al. (2018) for GDP and labour for NUTS identified in the study and located in the NE. In Northumberland and Tyne and Wear, the share of GDP exposed to Brexit is 12.2%, slightly higher than the share estimated for Tees Valley and Durham – 11.9%. In terms of local labour income exposure, estimates indicated a share 11.1% share for Northumberland and Tyne and Wear and 10.7% for Tees Valley and Durham. About one-third of GDP and labour shares identified in the two NE NUTS are associated with manufacturing: these figures are among the highest estimated for other UK NUTS and significantly higher compared to those estimates for EU NUTS, except for Irish regions.

Table 4.1.   UK Regional Shares of Local GDP and Labour Exposed to Brexit in Northern England.

NUTS2 Code	Name	GDP	Labour
UKC1	Tees Valley and Durham	11.9% (31.4%)	10.7% (31.3%)
UKC2	Northumberland Tyne and Wear	12.2% (35.5%)	11.1% (35.9%)
UKD1	Cumbria	16.3% (37.8%)	16.8% (37.8%)
UKD2	Cheshire	14.5% (38.4%)	13.0% (37.5%)
UKD3	Greater Manchester	11.3% (33.8%)	10.5% (34.4%)
UKD4	Lancashire	15.0% (39.0%)	14.5% (38.6%)
UKD5	Merseyside	10.4% (31.4%)	9.1% (31.8%)
UKE1	East Riding and North Lincolnshire	15.8% (39.0%)	15.1% (38.6%)
UKE2	North Yorkshire	13.4% (34.2%)	12.9% (34.6%)
UKE3	South Yorkshire	11.8% (34.7%)	11.1% (35.1%)
UKE4	West Yorkshire	12.1% (31.0%)	11.1% (31.4%)

Source: Author's elaboration from Chen et al. (2018).

IMPACT ACROSS ECONOMIC SECTORS IN THE NORTH EAST

The NE has traditionally been a major industrial region of England, despite perceptions of Northumberland as being predominantly rural. The presence of major manufacturers of non-British proprietorship, such as Nissan, Nestle and Komatsu, is significant. Manufacturing accounts for 14.8% of the region's total output and employs 9.6% of the region's workforce, with many more working in other associated industries and supply (North East Local Enterprise Partnership - NELEP, 2018b). Therefore, the implications of Brexit for manufacturing in general are of prime importance to the region.

Brexit also poses serious threats to digital organisations and start-ups, for instance those operating within creative industries. The Department for Culture, Media and Sport (DCMS, 2016) indicates that these companies account for one in 30 jobs (3.2%) in the NE, with about 66,000 working in the creative economy in the region. Creative industry companies face significant challenges including attracting and retaining highly skilled workers, as well as accessing financial support in the region (DCMS, 2016). Similarly, companies operating in the UK energy market are increasingly integrated with the EU single energy market: the potential changes to energy and climate policy resulting from Brexit (there had been 258 pieces of EU legislation within the 'energy acquis') pose a serious threat to the NE which boasts 48% of the UK's renewable power including 71% and 41% of UK wind power (NELEP, 2019a). Other companies, such as those operating in pharmaceutical and medical sectors, are also extremely exposed to Brexit. The NE has about 200 companies in the wider medicinal manufacturing industry, employing about 7,750 workers; the sector has built a strong reputation for regulatory expertise, high quality and a safe manufacturing record. There is a successful SME base working closely with industrial partners and a strong group of research and innovation assets in areas including formulation and biologics. The local life sciences and health care system in the region is very competitive and attracts significant investments from both UK and EU research funding bodies (NELEP, 2019a).

Changes affecting regulatory frameworks and levels of accessibility to the EU market would heavily affect the financial services sector. The sector represents the largest exporting industry of the UK, with a £67 billion contribution to the balance of trade, running a £18.5 billion trade surplus with the EU in 2014 (NELEP, 2019a). Financial services already provide over 2 million jobs to the UK economy, of which one-third based in London. Businesses in the NE are mainly located in Newcastle upon Tyne city centre and other key locations in the City of Durham, North Tyneside and at Sunderland. Part of these services serves to attract, develop and support infrastructural investments in the region, particularly regarding the main regional transport hubs: Newcastle upon Tyne International Airport and the five ports (Berwick, Blyth, Sunderland, Tyne and Seaham Harbour). In 2016, Newcastle International Airport accounted for nearly 2% (4.8 million passengers) of all the UK airport traffic with 66% of passengers travelling between Newcastle and EU destinations. In the same year, NE ports handled 5.73 million tonnes of freight – 1.2% of all freight handled in the UK, with. 584,000 passengers travelled through the Port of Tyne, equivalent to 2.7% of all international sea passengers boarding at UK ports (NELEP, 2019a).

The Brexit process and future outcomes are likely to have a significant impact on the UK higher education system too. UK universities are a major economic asset, generating an annual output of £73 billion for the British economy and contributing 2.8%

of UK GDP (Universities UK, 2017a, 2017b). In 2017, more than 17,000 international students attended programmes and courses delivered at the five NE universities (Durham, Newcastle, Northumbria, Sunderland and Teesside), with 14% of undergraduate students and 40% of postgraduate students coming from overseas. EU undergraduates and postgraduates at Northumbria and Newcastle Universities represent 3.4% and 6.3% of the universities' student population, respectively; these proportions are much higher when considering EU staff working at the two universities (7.7% at Northumbria and 18.9% at Newcastle). Aside universities, there are nine colleges in the NE; each of these works with an average of 600 businesses and trains an average of 1,200 apprentices per year, with nearly half of students advancing to higher level programmes (NELEP, 2019a).

Other NE economic key sectors for the generation of GVA, such as the public sector, hotels and restaurants, retail and tourism are inevitably exposed to Brexit. These sectors are particularly crucial in rural areas of the region: rural communities in the NE generate employment and economic growth, contributing to create and support vibrant industrial clusters and the service economy around urban and sub-urban centres (NELEP, 2019a). The interdependence of these sectors is likely to be accrued and exacerbated in relation to the differences that the Brexit process will create between UK and EU in commercial terms.

AUTOMOTIVE: THE MOST EXPOSED SECTOR?

With the wider manufacturing sector being a core part of the NE economy, the automotive sector deserves attention in view of possible Brexit scenarios. In the NE, the sector generates sales of over £11 billion annually and employs over 30,000 individuals within manufacturing companies and a further 141,000 jobs across UK supply chains (NELEP, 2018b). According to the NELEP, the NE region boasts the largest automotive cluster in the UK with over 250 companies and a predicted growth of over £3 billion by 2021. The Nissan plant at Sunderland is the UK largest car plant and one of the NE region's key employers – about 6,700 staff producing 2,000 cars a day (NELEP, 2018b). Investments in low carbon vehicle clusters are currently in phase of development and involve significant supply chain activities of national relevance, particularly in the Sunderland and South Tyneside area.

The automotive sector is a highly integrated global industry and has built its success on favourable trading conditions resulting from the UK's membership of the single market. Components in the EU supply chain in the car manufacturing process are moved from different state members numerous times before arriving at their final assembling point. This means that the Nissan car manufacturing plant at Sunderland may be receiving from and sending out various components across the channel up to four or five times to reach final output. If there were to be no free trade deal and tariffs were to be put on components both at entry and exit to the UK, the cost implications for car manufacturing in this country would be considerable. Given also that 60% of UK made cars are exported to the EU, the probable outcome of tariffs being imposed would be for car companies to move production abroad. However, a feasible outcome would be that reshoring would take place so that manufacturers in the supply chain in this country would see a boost to demand for their products and could possibly replace imported components (Cabras et al., 2018).

Whatever the case, the UK's withdrawal from the EU is likely to have a significant impact, if the introduction of new barriers to trade occurs, risking undermining the competitiveness of the sector. Nissan and other companies operating in the industry would have to reconfigure their supply chains, mainly in reference to potentially new costs related to trade barriers which would inevitably affect transport and logistics. However, the prolonged uncertainty associated with the negotiation process, with a possible exit from the EU postponed until end of October 2019, has already had an impact on decision affecting future investments in the NE. For instance, in February 2019, the company abandoned plans announced in 2016 to build a new model of one of its flagship vehicles, the X-Trail SUV, at its Sunderland plant, diverting the production to Japan instead. While the official statement released by the company indicated such a decision as a strategic business decision, the 'continued uncertainty around the UK's future relationship with the EU is not helping companies like ours to plan for the future' (Jones & Sabbagh, 2019).

The North East Independent Economic Review (NELEP, 2013) indicated the Nissan supply chain was worth about £1 billion for economy of the NE region. This figure could be representative of losses in case of a no deal Brexit, with significant repercussions in terms of disinvestments affecting the production of electric vehicles and other low carbon vehicles' technology (e.g. hydrogen, offshore wind turbines). Given the scale of the market, it is likely that losing free-barrier access to the EU market will affect and undermine hundreds of new jobs and apprenticeships in the NE.

CONCLUSIONS

The Brexit process and the UK/EU negotiation have already had an impact on the UK economy. The Withdrawal Agreement (WA) sealed by UK Prime Minister May with the European Commission has failed to get the approval from Parliament in three consecutive votes between January and March 2019, forcing the UK government to ask for an extension of the exit deadline originally set on 29 March 2019. The European Commission agreed to postpone this deadline to 12th April first, and then to 31st October once it was clear that a damaging no-deal exit was the only option available to the two parties. Meanwhile, Prime Minister May's resignation opened the way to a Conservative leadership contest in July 2019, with Boris Johnson becoming the new party leader and current Prime Minister; and EU elections in May 2019 have changed the composition of the EU Parliament, with newly elected members called to nominate new leaders of key EU institutions, including Commission, Council, Parliament and Central Bank.

At the time this chapter is being written, the Brexit scenario continues to be extremely fluid. The EU's present stance has not changed since the negotiation started: any talks on future trading agreements between the UK and EU will have to wait until a UK/EU for Brexit will be approved. However, with the negotiation phase now closed and May's WA already rejected by the UK Parliament, the European Commission has denied any possibility to re-open discussions regarding a new WA, further reducing the space for manoeuvring between the two parties. In such a context, the UK still formally remains an EU member state and, until the Brexit process is concluded, it is prohibited from making trade deals with other non-EU countries. This means that projections on growth and trade cannot be made.

However, the UK's ability to negotiate 'good' deals with non-EU members remains highly questionable. The claim made by the Leave campaign that 'once we are out of the EU, we will be able to negotiate whatever deal we want in the way we want' (citation from audience at a Brexit panel debate recorded in Carlisle; Cabras et al., 2018), is slowly fading away. Meetings held by UK representatives with representatives from larger economies in the past two years did not provide much information about how future relationships with any of the new potential commercial partners. For instance, a meeting between Prime Minister May and Indian Prime Minister Narendra Modi in September 2016 signalled that UK demands in terms of FDI needed to be matched by Indian requests of new visas for potential students, a trade-off likely to appear in many future negotiations with developing countries. Meanwhile, between 2016 and 2019, the EU finalised two important trade deals with Japan and the MERCOSUR, increasing to 38 the number of Free Trade Agreements (FTAs) hold with countries and blocs worldwide (involving a total of 65 sovereign nations) – all of which the UK will lose access to when exiting the EU.

A recent survey conducted by the NE Chamber of Commerce (North East England Chamber of Commerce, 2018) clearly identified businesses' current concerns in view of Brexit affecting immigration control, divergence from EU regulations and ability to strike independent trade deals. Surveyed businesses would prefer the UK remaining part of the single market and customs union, as this would minimise Brexit's impacts related to customs bureaucracy, economic tariffs and access to EU markets. Preparation for a no deal Brexit also needs to be considered, although the high levels of uncertainty and volatility associated with the Brexit process make planning for such scenario extremely challenging. In a survey conducted by the Confederation of British Institutes on over 300 businesses, 94% of respondents indicated that scenario planning is difficult because of lack of information available, while 77% say the number of potential scenarios increase the level of difficulty with future planning (Chamber of British Industries, 2018). Furthermore, about half of the surveyed businesses stated that making contingency plans presented prohibitive costs mainly due to the complexity of regulative frameworks and to the limited time available, which increased pressures (Chamber of British Industries, 2018).

In such a context, the NE faces significant challenges. Research conducted by Borchert and Temberi (2018) indicated that regions with the largest export values are not necessarily those that are most focussed on the EU, although some regions are more vulnerable to Brexit shocks due to the sectoral composition of their services, exporters and their orientation towards EU markets. The NE exports the most to EU countries overall, relative to non-EU destinations, similarly to other northern regions which export more to the EU than regions in the South. Furthermore, while the NE is the only UK region in which manufacturing experiences a continuing positive balance of trade with the EU (NELEP, 2019a) the sector in the region is heavily reliant on the EU for its export market (62% of total exports), making the trading relationship with the EU is extremely tight and complex in terms of supply chains. Equally important, the flux of skilled workers from other EU countries benefit NE manufacturers as it contributes to increase the quality of the workforce and to narrow the local skill-gap in terms of specialised knowledge. Import and export activities associated with manufacturing, as well as imports and exports related to other economic sectors in the NE (and more generally in the UK), benefit significantly from the EU's four freedoms: the free movement of goods, services, people and capital. For these reasons, businesses and companies in the region are very keen to maintain a tight relationship with the EU, securing access to both trade and resources with minimal disruption to the status quo (North East England Chamber of Commerce, 2018).

In conclusion, Brexit will undoubtedly affect the economy of the NE and the wider UK economic system, with important implications for decision-making processes regarding business strategies and investments in the region. Potential losses in terms of EU funding are likely to force NE local authorities to re-think previously made decisions based on uncertain future funding streams, and remediation or compensation for ceased EU support. Whatever Brexit will bring in terms of outcomes, a new, pan-regional approach involving industry and policy-makers from the NE and other Northern England regions appears to be urgently needed in order to increase efficiency and efficacy of (likely to be reduced) future resources and investments.

5

INDUSTRIAL STRATEGIES AND THE NORTH: WILL A LOCAL INDUSTRIAL STRATEGY DELIVER SOMETHING NEW?

David Charles

INTRODUCTION

For many decades the North of England, and particularly the North East, has been lagging economically behind the South East, a key reason being a relatively low level of innovation and industrial dynamism. Despite a history of innovation in the nineteenth century, the North of England languished during most of the twentieth century, as old industries and clusters declined and the region saw limited growth of innovation-intensive sectors, and particularly weak investment in the more research and development intensive parts of those sectors. The low levels of R&D, low levels of new firm formation and weaknesses in high technology sectors have been clear to see for many years, and public policy intervention has been urged for the last half century to address the problem, but with little real impact, as the gap with the south of England is getting worse. Back in the mid-1960s a report by the North of England Planning Council, 'The Challenge of the Changing North' called for greater investment in R&D and universities to stimulate innovative industries, and many other reports since then have made similar points, yet change, when it has come, has been insufficient to achieve convergence with the South.

The current position, facing the prospect of leaving the EU presents the region with considerable challenges. Despite the growth of new industries in recent years, the North East still lags behind other regions, and is more dependent on export-oriented manufacturing industries, such as the automotive sector which face decline post-Brexit. Yet at the same time government has rediscovered the need for an industrial policy and has asked regions to develop their own local industrial strategies. Does this present an opportunity for the North East, and if so what should the region do in that strategy?

KEY WEAKNESSES: URBAN STRATEGIC FUNCTIONS AND R&D

The central challenge for the region has been to find ways of attracting and developing new industries to replace those that have declined, while national neoliberal-inspired policy has facilitated the loss of capabilities from the traditional industries and their more rapid decline while offering branch plant operations in both manufacturing and services to replace them. Thus, traditional engineering businesses with design capabilities vanished in the early 1980s to be replaced with assembly plants drawing on design and innovation capabilities from elsewhere, usually overseas. Both the traditional industries and the branch operations that replaced them have not been ideal as sources of entrepreneurial talent and ideas, so the remedy for decline has further weakened the region, and left it with little response when more recent foreign direct investments were relocated from the North to other parts of Europe, or to Asia.

Related to the relative lack of innovation has been the weakness of the North's cities relative to similar sized cities elsewhere in Europe. Urban agglomeration is seen as beneficial in the development of knowledge-based industries and services (OECD, 2009, 2010), but the North's cities lack the kind of strategic high-level functions that are to be found in competitor cities: headquarters, international financial service firms, central or regional government (Swinney, 2016). In response to this, the Northern Powerhouse has sought to create scale by better connecting and integrating the North's cities, thereby stimulating demand for new services.

What has been needed to respond to these issues is a strategic approach that goes beyond regional aid but seeks to reinvigorate the industrial structure of the North, through a form of industrial policy: rebuilding new industries and finding ways of re-using the remaining skills of the old. But industrial policy went out of favour for several decades as neoliberalism became the dominant ideology. Indeed, governments have overseen a steady decline in R&D in the UK from a level of around 2.2% of GDP in the early 1980s to a current level of less than 1.7%, well below the EU average of 2.07% and below the current UK target of 2.4%. Part of this decline has been a reduction in government R&D performance through defence R&D cuts after the end of the Cold War, the privatisation of former public corporations such as in energy (where the new private owners reduced R&D expenditure) and the closure or privatisation of public research establishments (Jones, 2018). So, while university research expenditure has increased and government is now investing more in supporting research in the private sector, there has been a long period of under-investment within which the needs of the North have been further neglected.

THE INDUSTRIAL STRATEGY REVIVAL

Since the start of the current century, industrial policy has been on the return. Labour had a tacit industrial policy through its support for regional development agencies and their sectoral and cluster strategies, as well as through the Technology Strategy Board and support for nationally strategic sectors such as the auto industry post-2007. This was particularly important in the North where Regional Development Agencies (RDAs) invested heavily in innovation projects targeted at developing new sectors, with some success. In the North East, the RDA identified key sectors and clusters such as energy, process industries and life sciences and used both RDA and European Regional Development Fund (ERDF) support to develop new research and translational innovation activities, some of which has continued in the form of Catapult centres to support key technologies nationally. Nissan also benefited from RDA support for manufacturing, and from Gordon Brown's interventions to assist the car industry during the global financial crisis. While the RDAs were abolished under the Coalition government, industrial strategy continued its re-emergence under Vince Cable as Business Secretary.

A key development was Michael Heseltine's 'No Stone Unturned' report (Heseltine, 2012), which focussed on national growth and particularly sustainable growth in all regions. A central focus was localism and the devolution of power and funding to local leaders to develop tailored solutions building on existing local strengths, but Heseltine also called for a strong dialogue between government and key industrial sectors. The nascent industrial strategy which has emerged focussed on key issues such as finance, sectoral partnerships, technology development, skills, and government procurement. George Osborne's Northern Powerhouse proposal followed in 2014.

Some initial investment followed, although the story as seen from the North East has been a little disappointing. Manchester has received a £235 million commitment for a new Royce Institute for Advanced Materials Research and Innovation – what might be considered the answer to his question in 2014 as to what will be the 'Crick' of the North (referring to the need for an equivalent to the London-based Francis Crick Institute, a new £700 million building to house 1,250 life science researchers). The North East however has been less well supported. More recent investments in National Innovation Centres in Newcastle for data and for ageing have received around £35 million of government funding support.

At a local level the RDAs were replaced by the Local Enterprise Partnerships (LEPs) with the old North East region being split between two LEPs – Tees Valley and a remainder North East LEP area. Despite increased resources being made available for the LEPs following the Heseltine report, there is relatively limited strategic capacity in what remain quite small organisations, which are thus very dependent on the support of regional partners. Local authorities have however also lost strategic capacity as a result of austerity cuts. Universities remain important local players, especially in innovation policy, but have faced other challenges around their performance against national parameters in the Research Excellence Framework and Teaching Excellence Framework, and in many cases pulled back from ERDF projects in their local regions due to increased regulatory risk and the absence of matched funding. LEPs produced Strategic Economic Plans in partnership with their local stakeholders, but these often lacked detail and identified broad priority sectors which often reflected previous RDA clusters.

Following the referendum on EU membership, the context for industrial policy shifted. On the one hand there was an increased need for a more radical industrial policy to respond to the challenges (or opportunities if more optimistically inclined) that would face the UK in losing access to the Single Market. The appointment of Greg Clark as Theresa May's Secretary of State for Business, Energy and Industrial Strategy gave a boost to the industrial strategy concept after some indifference from his predecessor Sajid Javid. On the other hand, the resignation of Cameron led to the sacking of George Osborne and a reduced emphasis on the Northern Powerhouse.

All of this set the scene for the launch of a new UK industrial Strategy in November 2017 (Department for Business, Energy and Industrial Strategy (BEIS), 2017). The national strategy draws together several aspects of policy to support UK-wide competitiveness. Much of this is generic such as skills, infrastructure and the business environment, but there is an identification of place as an underpinning factor and an emphasis of delivery through sector deals. How then do we regionalise this industrial strategy in ways in which it helps to diversify and rebuild the economies of the North?

WHAT WILL A LOCAL INDUSTRIAL STRATEGY ACHIEVE FOR THE NORTH EAST REGION?

The proposed solution is the development of Local Industrial Strategies (LIS) by LEPs in each part of England in partnership with their localities, universities and the private sector.

A key question is how these local industrial strategies fit with the national strategy. As the national strategy was developed first as a top down approach, then local strategies are to some extent constrained by this. Local strategies must somehow capture opportunities based on local assets, but still connect with national priorities, so there is an implicit message that local priorities should reflect national priorities. A national strategy that sought to support the sum of local strategies would probably look quite different.

These local industrial strategies are emerging through a slow rolling process of commissioning across three tranches so far. An initial tranche of published reports includes the West the last two decades Midlands and Greater Manchester, but also three LISs related to the Oxford to Cambridge axis, and the West of England (focussed on Bristol). These are quite boosterish documents identifying strengths and opportunities, listing recent investments and pointing to positive developments for the future. What they do not do, although this may be in unpublished documents, is present a realistic analysis of the sources of weakness of the regional economy, the threats from Brexit and other challenges, and how the proposed actions will lead to a change in those underlying problems. These initial local strategies are also all in stronger regions with a well-developed research base, so it will be interesting to see what happens in some of the so-called left behind regions where there is less recent investment to shout about.

WE NEED TO BUILD ON PREVIOUS EUROPEAN EXPERIENCE

These new local industrial strategies should be building on of innovation strategies at the regional level. The first of these strategies were developed in the mid-1990s with funding from the EU. Initially Regional Technology Plans were launched as pilot actions by DG XVI (now DG Regio), followed by mainstream programmes from the same DG as Regional Innovation Strategies, and by the then DG for innovation (DGXIII) which launched Regional Innovation and Technology Transfer Strategies (RITTS) (Charles, Nauwelaers, Mouton, & Bradley, 2000). Not all UK regions (or sub-regions) took up this support, but those that did included Wales, North East, East Midlands, Dorset/Hampshire, Kent, North London, Oxfordshire, Highlands and Islands, West Midlands, Strathclyde and Yorkshire/Humberside. These strategy initiatives aimed to identify the strengths and weaknesses of regional innovation capacity, propose means to better match supply and demand for technology, and identify projects that could be supported by the Structural Funds.

These were followed by a UK requirement for English RDAs to have regional innovation strategies, building on a lead established initially by the three northern English regions in response to the low level of R&D, and the specific incidence of the proposed closure of the Daresbury Lab near Manchester (Charles, Perry, & Benneworth, 2004). Soon after, six science cities were also launched, the first three being in the three Northern regions – Newcastle, York and Manchester (Charles & Wray, 2015). Throughout there has been an ongoing requirement for regions to have programme strategies in place for the EU Structural Funds, with a gradual shift over time in emphasis towards innovation and enterprise actions. During the 2000s these were integrated with the RDA sectoral and innovation priorities. The European Commission's encouragement of knowledge-based development through the Structural Funds culminated in the requirement for all 2014–2020 programmes to incorporate a Regional Innovation Strategy for Smart Specialisation.

SMART SPECIALISATION

Smart specialisation is particularly relevant to discussions of an industrial policy and the need to rebuild sectors and clusters in the North, as the aim is to identify new investment projects have priorities that can form the basis of emerging industries, but which are rooted in the existing skills and knowledge base of the region. However, the UK does not seem to have taken smart specialisation very seriously in its current European Structural and Investment Funds (ESIF) programmes, even though these were developed prior to the EU referendum. A national smart specialisation hub was created to share experience, but on the ground, projects have been drawn from local capabilities in regions that have been stripped of the strategic capacity embodied in the RDAs. The big problem for England was the decision of the Coalition government to shift away from regional ERDF programmes to a single programme for England (although Scotland, Wales and Northern Ireland have their own programmes). The English ESIF programme had to develop a uniform framework for a diverse set of regional circumstances, but then deliver support via the 38 LEPs, each of which was given a share of the English budget and expected to develop local programmes linking with their Strategic Economic Plans. This led to the rather clumsy structure of a smart specialisation strategy at English level which largely focussed on identifying some science strengths and priorities at national level and key regional sectoral clusters, with diverse local level programmes which also sought to identify their own sectoral strengths and growth opportunities.

Consequently, local either tended to strongly connect with national priorities in order to obtain support from UK funds, or else develop on a generic non-specialised basis to meet the diverse needs of local firms. This does not seem to fit with the spirit of smart specialisation and since the referendum there has been little interest in such a European concept.

One attempt to try and identify local innovation strengths was the regional Science and Innovation Audits, launched by Jo Johnson in 2015 and undertaken between 2015 and 2018. These were intended to 'help local organisations map their research and innovation strengths and identify areas of potential global competitive advantage' (BEIS, 2015). The call for the audits recognised the need to make better use of existing data to be combined with local knowledge in identifying opportunities (BEIS, 2016). Three 'waves' of audits were funded, with local research organisations leading on the audits around specific sectoral or scientific themes with varying geographies – some regional, some sub-regional and some pan-regional. Particularly in the case of the pan-regional examples the geographies sometimes only related to the specific technologies, such as the Offshore Renewables audit which covered the LEPs for Humber, Liverpool City Region, North East and Tees Valley, plus Scottish Enterprise. The problem with this approach though is that the audits focussed on the identification of local innovation and industrial strengths and offered very little for those regions whose problem was the absence of such strengths. Throughout, all the proposed policy solutions for the lagging regions have been to identify strengths that can be further developed, and the idea of seeding new activities in regions without such strengths has been anathema.

POST-BREXIT PLANS

With the proposed departure of the UK from the EU and the loss of the EU Structural Funds, the UK government has proposed a replacement fund called the Shared Prosperity Fund (SPF). However, now there are few details available, despite repeated government promises of a consultation process. The SPF is intended to replace the Structural Funds and address the disparities between regions in the UK and 'help deliver sustainable, inclusive growth based on our modern industrial strategy' (Brien, 2019). Without clarification on the way the SPF will operate it is unclear how this funding will relate to the emerging local industrial strategies, although it may be assumed that the SPF could be the main vehicle for funding new priorities identified by the LIS.

The scale of investment required in regions such as the North East if they are to see convergence with national levels of economic performance is large. Over the years of Structural Funds support the gap has not narrowed significantly, although there was some slight convergence in the early 2000s with high levels of both ERDF and RDA spending (Charles & Michie, 2013). There must be concern then that the SPF will not provide the level of investment needed and indeed it may not even match the level of funding from the Structural Funds combined with national funding such as through the various Growth Funds distributed via LEPs in recent years.

Another major concern is whether funds will be allocated to regions according to need or whether there will be some form of competition in which the poorest regions (perhaps those left behind or which 'don't matter' (Rodriguez-Pose, 2019) will lose out to better organised regions with projects that offer better returns on investment.

STRENGTH IN PLACES?

In advance of the SPF government has also launched a programme called Strength in Places, which aims to support innovation-led regional growth through support for research-based activities involving universities and businesses around regional clusters. In a sense this is much closer to smart specialisation than much of what has been supported through the ERDF.

Table 5.1.   Strength in Places Bids 2019.

Wales	1	Semiconductors.
Northern Ireland	1	Maritime transportation.
Scotland	4	Industrial biotechnology, nanofabrication, fintech, precision medicine.
North East	3	Automotive, green hydrogen, ageing.
North West	2	Materials chemistry, infectious disease prevention and treatment.
Yorkshire and Humber	3	Renewable energy, glass, medical technologies.
East Midlands	1	Rehabilitation medicine.
West Midlands	1	Medical technologies.
South West	3	Cyber business (with Wales), environmental intelligence, screen-based media.
London	1	Performing arts.
East of England	2	Agriculture, logistics/supply chain.
South East	1	Agri-food.

Source: BEIS (2019).

There are currently 23 shortlisted projects from the first wave of applications.

The Strength in Places Fund builds also on the set of previous initiatives such as the science and innovation audits as some of the target sectors emerge from these. Again, the emphasis is on rewarding existing success, although there is a tacit acknowledgement that funding for the weaker regions should be a priority given the focus on narrowing regional disparities. Whether this is reflected in the final selection of projects is yet to be seen. With a likelihood of only six or so projects to be funded in the first tranche then it begs the question of why London and the South East were even allowed to bid if the aim was to help rebalance the regions.

SO, WHAT SHOULD THE LOCAL INNOVATION
STRATEGIES DO?

The emphasis of the local innovation strategies so far seems to be on identifying existing plans for innovation investment and aiming to increase regional productivity, but surely there should be more to these strategies than this? A key aim should be to rebuild the economic base of the disadvantaged regions – this might then facilitate higher levels of productivity, but a rebalanced economy needs to see dramatic changes to the spatial distribution of high value activities, rather than local tinkering. The What Works Centre for Local Economic Development has suggested that one thing LEPs shouldn't do is to set ambitious high-level targets for growth in GDP or increases in productivity (What Works Centre for Local Economic Growth, 2018). These tend not to be particularly effective, don't drive change, and are usually characterised mainly by the fact that they are wildly ambitious and never achieved. Almost 30 years of ERDF programmes in the North East have demonstrated the inability of the region to set meaningful achievable targets, and a tendency for such things to be derailed by external shocks (Charles & Michie, 2013). Similarly, the What Works Centre suggests that benchmarking against national averages doesn't tell us much as any national figures are dominated by the effect of London and the South East. What is needed instead is a much more granular understanding of the effects and opportunities of new technologies and business model innovations on the specific mix of industries, firms and capabilities of the regions. In this sense the previous analysis of regional innovation systems and the science and innovation audits provide a foundation, as does the concept of smart specialisation with a focus on identifying entrepreneurial opportunities for regional firms and partners to develop new growing industries. These may fit within nationally identified grand challenges but may also diverge from national strategies if the region has a distinctive capability. After all innovation is about identifying something new, which may not have been identified in national top down strategies?

The focus for the North East LIS should be on the real problems and opportunities facing the North East. The problems of the region are largely the same problems faced over the past 40 years – low levels of innovation and productivity and poor social conditions as a result. However, to achieve real change, relative to the national average, it is not sufficient for the region to identify targets or priorities; there needs to be a national commitment to kick-starting the development of the region with a clear objective to see the region grow faster than the more affluent regions of the South. Without that commitment it is unlikely that a region with fewer assets is going to be able to narrow the gap on the South East.

6

BREXIT AND DEVOLUTION: A VIEW FROM 'NORTH OF TYNE' AND THE ANGLO-SCOTTISH 'BORDERLANDS'

Keith Shaw

*It's not the despair. I can take the despair. It's the
hope I can't stand.*

> *(Brian Stimpson, played by John Cleese
> in the film,* Clockwise, *1986)*

INTRODUCTION

The shadow of Brexit looms ominously over any discussion of contemporary political institutions and processes in the UK. Suitably uncertain – not to say gloomy – pronouncements thus characterise much of the recent literature on Devolved Governance within England.

On one level, these capture the challenges faced by local councils whose risk registers have to confront, for example, the end of EU funding, reduction in the number of EU workers in key sectors, the introduction of new procurement regimes and the need for a new legal basis for some public services (House of Commons, 2019). While on another level, there are concerns about the fate of the overall devolution process in England where there are fears that recent attempts (via 'Devolution Deals') to give local communities greater power and control over their futures will suffer as Brexit forces the Government to actually go against its own devolution agenda (McCann & Ortego-Argiles, 2019)

Such critical judgement on the impact of the Brexit process on recent developments in sub-national governance in England can also be added to the initial concerns expressed over the Government's plans to encourage the setting up of a number of new Combined Local Authorities, with directly elected mayors, new powers and resources (British Academy, 2017). Several assessments concluded that such deals lacked clear overarching democratic principles, were conducted behind closed doors, didn't offer enough resources or powers to tackle regional inequalities and created new 'artificial' boundaries (see e.g. Pike, Kempton, Marlow, O'Brien, & Tomaney, 2016; Tomaney, 2018).

Without resorting to platitudes on 'never wasting a good crisis' or underplaying the considerable challenges posed by Brexit, it can also be argued that there are still opportunities in the present climate to develop new innovative approaches to sub-national governance. Approaches that continue to highlight both the resilience of local government in responding to crises (Shaw, 2012) and the flexibilities remaining to reshape – from the bottom-up – the boundaries of traditional place-based approaches to economic development.

As an illustration, this chapter focusses on the development of new sub-national governance arrangements in the North of England and in the Scottish Borders. These developments, encompassing both the Borderlands Growth Deal and the North of Tyne Combined Authority (CA), illustrate how there is mileage still left in the devolution agenda in England and how Brexit, in some cases, has actually allowed 'space' for such developments to be conceived and redeveloped. In this sense at least, the challenge is to recognise that there are some hopeful signs even among the despair.

BREXIT AND THE DEVOLUTION AGENDA

The contemporary devolution agenda within England was formed (and developing momentum) well before the 2016 referendum on EU membership. Reflecting the Coalition Government's rejection of the regional tier of governance, the 2011 Localism Act gave ministers the power to transfer responsibilities to individual cities that came forward with innovative proposals to promote economic growth.

One feature of the Act was to promote a 'City Deal' process that would see, in exchange for being granted greater powers, several English cities and their wider areas assuming responsibility for delivering growth locally (National Audit Office, 2015). The first wave of City Deals covered the eight largest cities (including Manchester, Birmingham and Newcastle) that were in the Core Cities Group. A further, second, wave of 20 City Deal agreements then encompassed the next 14 largest cities, plus the six cities with the highest population growth between 2001 and 2010. These included smaller city regions such as Greater Cambridge, Oxford and Oxfordshire, Tees Valley, and Hull and the Humber (Cabinet Office, 2013).

Following the May 2015 General Election, the new Conservative Government further revised the approach by announcing an additional 'Devolution Deal' which allowed combined bodies made up of a number of councils to ask for additional responsibilities and funding as long as they agreed to accept the introduction of a directly elected mayor for the new CA (House of Commons, 2015).

However, for some commentators, the entire devolution process has now been derailed by Brexit:

> *The need to control the complex process of delivering Brexit has meant that the Westminster government has excluded sub national government from almost all Brexit-related negotiations. On top of this, the government agenda aimed at enhancing sub-national devolution, which began in earnest in 2014, has almost entirely stalled .... The ad hoc, uncoordinated and largely powerless responses of local government to Brexit demonstrate the UK's sub-national power vacuum in this crucial arena.*
> *(McCann & Ortego-Argiles, 2019, p. 47)*

Preparing for Brexit has clearly created turmoil at a subnational level already dealing with austerity, sluggish economic growth and limited funding to prepare for Brexit. Nor have senior local council leaders, including the elected mayors in our largest cities, been adequately engaged in wider negotiations on Brexit.

However, there is an alternative case to be made that while the pace of devolution initiatives may have slowed, they have not completely stalled. Indeed, preparations for Brexit have, arguably, allowed space for locally crafted plans for greater devolution to be developed and legitimised and added momentum to more radical calls for greater devolution in a post-Brexit UK. There is also an argument that following the EU referendum there is greater policy attention devoted to rural areas, coastal communities and smaller towns excluded from the bulk of devolution opportunities so far.

Indeed, there may be an argument that with Central Government transfixed by the Brexit process, there are opportunities to push ahead with locally inspired plans. Tony Travers (2017) has argued that,

> As Theresa May's government starts the complex process of renegotiating the UK's relationship with the rest of the world, Whitehall seems likely to be distracted from domestic policy for several, possibly many, years. Devolution to city and county-regions offers her government an opportunity to concentrate its efforts elsewhere.

We may even be witnessing the start of a (slight) shift back towards local government being viewed – in Jim Bulpit's (1983) famous distinction – as 'low' politics rather than 'high'. A key feature of the former being that, for the most part, central elites kept out of local administration and let elected councils deal with local issues in their own way.

Thus, despite the earlier view (above) that the Devolution agenda in England has stalled since 2016, there are still clear signs of life.

As discussed in the next section, the North of Tyne CA has recently joined the seven other combined bodies with elected mayors (May 2019) and after much-wrangling, agreement has been reached on plans by the four councils within the Sheffield CA (PSE, 26/3/2019).

Other more traditional 'deals' (not involving an elected mayor) continue to be announced – such as the Borderlands Growth Deal (BBC, 2019) which will be discussed in the next section.

Proposals for the setting up of unitary councils to replace county and district bodies (in former two-tier areas) have been accepted in Dorset (Conrad, 2019) and Buckinghamshire, as have moves to reduce the number of district councils in Somerset. Talks are also underway to move towards unitary councils in several other two-tier areas.

Despite ongoing criticism (particularly of the former) the two pan-regional 'growth machines', the 'Northern Powerhouse' and the 'Midlands Engine' continue to provide at least a vehicle for collaborative approaches. In the meantime, interest continues, in rescaling in terms of a more permanent pan-regional Council for the North (Cox, 2017)

In the context of Brexit, there are also more fundamental debates and ideas on the future of the UK. Whether – within a Federal Britain – the governance of England is best served by the creation of an English Parliament (Russell & Sheldon, 2018) or by revisiting arguments about the merits of directly elected institutions at the regional level (Blick, 2019). Lord Heseltine has also made a strong case for creating a new Central Government Department of the Regions and restoring government offices in the regions in addition to increasing the powers of the CAs (Heseltine, 2019).

On the ground, the new directly elected mayors are beginning to carve out a niche for themselves and interest in expanding this role continues. This is both in terms of exercising their powers (the Tees Valley Mayor has recently pushed through the 'municipalisation' of the ailing Tees Valley Airport: Northern Echo, 4/12/2018) and in making the case out for greater devolution to meet the challenges of Brexit (Burnham, 2019). As one review of the mayoral role argues:

> Brexit will reshape the UK economy and society, as well as how the nation is governed. There is a strong case to introduce mayors in other English cities and to allow them to take a greater role in political life. Elected mayors could, for example,

> *have an important role working with central*
> *government to determine what powers might be*
> *repatriated to a local level, after Brexit .... There is*
> *also scope for elected mayors to influence national*
> *and global debates by acting as a united force to*
> *demand greater devolution after Brexit. (Ayres &*
> *Beer, 2018)*

One feature of the 2016 Referendum vote was the large 'Leave' vote in smaller towns, coastal communities and rural areas outside the main urban conurbations – the so-called 'revenge of the places that don't matter' (Pike, 2018). This has strengthened the case for greater policy attention being paid to areas outside the present CAs to stem what one account has called 'the politics of resent-ment' (Jennings, Stoker, & Warren, 2019). This also chimes with previous criticisms of the Devolution Deal Process for ignoring the needs of rural economies (IPPR North, 2017) and failing to develop the type of coordinated and strategic approach to rural governance and productivity on offer to largely urban CAs.

The next section will provide an illustration of some of these themes by looking at the North East of England, where the political 'space' partly created by Brexit has encour-aged some councils to consider new and flexible place-based approaches to devolution that may not have been possible under 'normal' circumstances. This also reminds us of the continuing importance of the local political dimension in cre-ating and reshaping boundaries where functional economic geographies – devised by national policy-makers – fail to map on to the new and emerging challenges and opportunities. Such proactive approaches also show that 'local and regional actors are not passive, nor do they simply respond to the ini-tiatives of the centre' (Pike & Tomaney, 2009, p. 29).

'SOME ORDER OUT OF CHAOS': THE BORDERLANDS AND NORTH OF TYNE

On the surface at least, the impact of post-2010 devolution initiatives in the North East could be viewed as producing more
fragmented and cluttered governance arrangements. The aboli-
tion of the North East Region (its Development Agency and
Government Office), the creation of two Local Enterprise Partnerships (covering the North and South of the region) and the
plans to create two new Combined Authorities (CA) – based
on the same North–South demarcation – created considerable
upheaval and the loss of a coherent regional 'voice'. Indeed, the
subsequent failure of the seven Councils in the 'North' of the
North East (as the North East Combined Authority (NECA))
to agree to be designated (as Tees Valley had) as a formal CA
with an elected mayor, further added to the complexity – and
confusion (Shaw & Robinson, 2018).

The political impasse created by the inability of council leaders to agree on a Devolution deal for the North of
the region, was also the product of the uncertainty produced by both referenda in this period – the 2014 poll on
Scottish Independence and the 2016 EU membership vote.
The former concentrated minds in the North East on the
potential implications for the region of their 'nearest neigh-
bours' becoming independent (Shaw, 2018), while the latter
activated a number of concerns from local councils on
undermining trading relations with Europe, reductions in
EU funding, the drying up of the pool of EU workers and
concerns about specific sectors, including the car industry
and the large rural sector in the region (Cabras et al., 2017).

When faced with this uncertainty, some North East Councils (including both senior councillors and officials) supported by a range of stakeholders (including local business
and the higher education sector) have viewed the changed
devolutionary circumstances as providing real opportunities

for new forms of innovative political and administrative joint working.

On the one hand, with councils on both sides of the Anglo-Scottish border, via the Borderlands Growth Deal (Fig. 6.1) and between urban and rural authorities in the 'North of the Tyne' CA (Fig. 6.2).

The latter, CA, sees Newcastle, North Tyneside and North-umberland forming North of Tyne, which now has to coexist with the remaining North East councils in NECA and the councils in the Tees Valley CA. As Figure 6.2. shows

- The North of Tyne CA is made up of areas 1 (Northumberland), 2(a) Newcastle and 2(c) North Tyneside. Areas 2(b), 2(d), 2(e) and 3 make up the separate NECA Councils. Areas 4–8 make up the Tees Valley CA.

- The remaining NECA Councils are: Gateshead (2b), South Tyneside (2d), Sunderland (2e) and Durham (3).

- The Tees Valley CA councils are: Darlington (4), Hartlepool (5), Stockton (6), Redcar & Cleveland (7) and Middlesbrough (8).

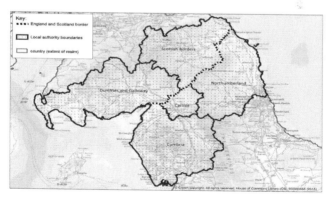

Fig. 6.1. The Borderland's Deal Local Authorities.

Source: House of Commons (2015). Contains Parliamentary Information Licensed under the Open Parliament License v3.0.

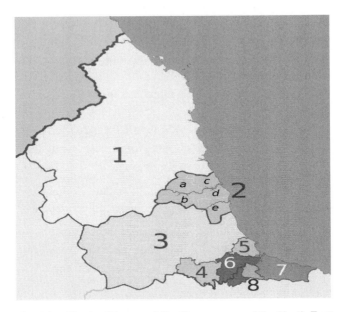

Fig. 6.2.   North of Tyne and the Governance of the North East.

Source: Dr Greg and Nilfanion. Contains Ordnance Survey data © Crown Copyright and Database Right 2011.

As of March 2019, both the UK and Scottish Governments have recognised and committed resources to the Borderlands Inclusive Growth Deal. As one former minister noted,

> *I hope other areas can show the same*
> *persuasiveness to enable the government to show*
> *it is serious about rebalancing the economy and*
> *creating opportunities for the young and for*
> *businesses. (O'Neill, quoted in LGC, 2019)*

On the 1st July, the key Government Ministers and Local Council leaders from both sides of the Border signed the Heads of Terms that sees the five councils add an additional £45m to the deal, taking the overall amount to £394.5m

(GOV.UK, 2019). While the creation and development of the original Borderlands Partnership has been covered elsewhere (see e.g., Shaw et al., 2014), Box 6.1 captures its main features and distinctiveness – including the north–south and east–west linkages and placing rural development at the core of plans for inclusive growth.

BOX 6.1. The Borderlands Growth Deal.

The Partners: The Borderlands Partnership brings together for the first time the five cross-border local authorities – Carlisle City Council, Cumbria County Council, Dumfries and Galloway Council, Northumberland County Council and Scottish Borders Council.

Development: Discussions between the main councils and relevant Government Departments on both sides of the border began in earnest following the 2013 publication of the Borderlands Report which identified the common opportunities and challenges facing councils on both sides of the Border and articulated the case for using the independence debate to stimulate cross-border initiatives given the centralised polity and unbalanced economy dominated by London and the wider South East (ANEC, 2013).

Common challenges: Include a large proportion of their populations living in rural areas, which provide challenges in relation to accessibility, connectivity with regard to broadband and mobile infrastructure, transport infrastructure and the economic future of market towns; particular problems with low level of wealth creation, low pay, a lack of representation of high growth economic sectors, the outmigration of young people and an ageing population (The Borderlands Proposition, 2017)

Common assets: Include a population of over 1 million people and incorporates almost 10% of land area of Great Britain; high levels of self-employment in the area and the growth in micro and small businesses are opportunities which could be exploited; opportunities to develop energy production, both on and off shore, and adding value to the tourism product; Just under 25% of the workforce work in agricultural, forestry and fishing businesses: a sector that provides a potential opportunity given the change in consumer demands for higher quality, locally sourced, produce over mass production (Shaw et al., 2015).

The Plan: The Borderlands Inclusive Growth Plan has six key programmes: Digital, Borderlands Energy Investment Company, Destination Borderlands, Quality of Place, Knowledge Exchange Network and Business Infrastructure Programme (Scottish Borders Council, 2018). Many of its strategies highlight the rural context of development.

The Deal: In July 2019, the Scottish and UK Governments announced combined investment of £394.5m in the Borderlands. The £85 million over 10 years from the former, £260m from the latter, and £45m from the five councils themselves. The Deal aims to deliver over 5,500 jobs, dramatically improve transport and digital connectivity, boost tourism and generate around £1.1 billion of economic benefits for the region (BBC, 2019).

Key Projects:

- Up to £19 million for a world class mountain bike innovation centre in the Scottish Borders.

- Up to £5 million for the development of the Lilidorei play village at Alnwick Gardens, a year-round visitor attraction to boost local economic growth.

- Up to £10 million joint funding with Scottish Government to assess the feasibility of extending the Borders Railway from Tweedbank to Carlisle.

- Up to £15 million in improvements at Carlisle railway station, as the largest station in the Borderlands, to enhance connectivity and access into the wider Borderlands region.

- Up to £16.2 million in the South of Scotland to improve digital connectivity.

- Up to £7.8 million to the development of a new business and employment site at Chapelcross, a former nuclear power station in Dumfries and Galloway.

- Up to £4 million to support research and innovation in the dairy industry.

Alongside new developments across the Anglo-Scottish border, new sub-national arrangements have also recently emerged 'North of Tyne' as the new body elected its first mayor in May 2019. Forced to confront the leadership conflicts, territorial antagonisms and arguments over the acceptance of an elected sub-regional mayor, three of the North of England Combined Authority (NECA) councils (Newcastle, North Tyneside and Northumberland) split off and went on to negotiate their own 'Devo-Deal' with Government (Box 6.2). This now leaves the other four local authorities (Durham, Gateshead, South Tyneside and Sunderland) as the remaining partners of the original NECA.

BOX 6.2. The North of Tyne Combined Authority.

The Partners: Newcastle, North Tyneside and Northumberland local authorities. First two council Labour controlled, the last, Conservative. Labour mayor elected in May 2019. The CA board comprises the mayor, council leaders and deputy leaders and the chair of the North East Local Enterprise Partnership (NELEP).

The Area: It begins at the most southerly boundary of Northumberland and continues north to the border with Scotland, and spans from the North Sea on the east coast to the border with Cumbria in the west. The area has a population of 880,000, a local economy of £17 billion, over 360,000 jobs and it is home to 23,000 businesses.

Challenges: Consistently higher unemployment than the national average, lower productivity than the national average, social inequality with pockets of deprivation and a lack of job opportunities in some areas.

Opportunities: One of the fastest growing technology sectors outside of London; the highest skilled workforce in the North; excellent transport links nationally and internationally; innovation, research and development hubs in two universities and world-leading businesses; a huge range of natural, historic and cultural assets (North of Tyne, 2018).

The Deal:

- Control of a £20 million per year allocation of revenue funding, over 30 years (£650m) to be invested by the Mayor-led North of Tyne CA to drive growth and take forward its economic priorities.

- Establishment of an Inclusive Growth Board, with Government participation, to better integrate skills and employment programmes across the area, including a North of Tyne Education Improvement Challenge.

- Driving improvements to rural growth and productivity, and becoming a Rural Business Scale up Champion for England.

- Devolution of the Adult Education Budget for the area to allow North of Tyne to shape local skills provision to respond to local needs.

- Establishment of a Housing and Land Board, with powers to the CA to acquire and dispose of land, and mayoral powers to take forward compulsory purchases and establish Mayoral Development Corporations, as a foundation for North of Tyne's housing and regeneration ambition.

- Collaborative working with Government to support North of Tyne in taking forward its considerable ambitions around digital capability and infrastructure, and low-carbon energy.

- Create a statutory Joint Committee to exercise transport jointly on behalf of the North of Tyne and NECAs.

What is also noticeable in the new council's mission statement is a realistic emphasis on Brexit and the wider challenges:

> *Brexit will, of course, present both opportunities*
> *and challenges; we need to negotiate a new*
> *relationship with Europe and ensure that we*
> *continue to have the skills base needed for*
> *businesses to thrive. But there are longer term*
> *challenges too, such as increasing automation, an*
> *ageing society and the global need to tackle climate*
> *change. (North of Tyne, 2018)*

It is also clear that the aim to become, 'a national exemplar for rural growth and stewardship' means that the New CA will not only produce a North of Tyne Rural Productivity Plan but also work across the 'wider North East and Borderland geographies, including via the emerging Borderlands Growth Deal' (DHCLG, 2018, p 20). Evidence, on the ground at least, that some order and coherence is also emerging across different local jurisdictions and devolution deals.

CONCLUSIONS: GROUNDS FOR HOPE?

Despite the challenges and uncertainties created by Brexit at the sub-national level, the process has not completely derailed moves towards devolution within England. Indeed, the pressures of Brexit on Central Government have both created a political space for local initiatives to act in a proactive and creative manner and allowed a new generation of local leaders to argue that for Brexit to succeed, greater devolution is needed. In this sense, Brexit has served to strengthen the case for localism:

> *In the longer term, there is also now a unique*
> *opportunity to re-evaluate the distribution of*
> *powers between central and local government and*

> determine how greater devolution can be used to
> obtain the best possible outcomes for people and
> communities. (House of Commons, 2019, p. 16)

Moreover, as the exemplar of the North East of England also illustrates, the two new developments in sub-national governance – the Borderlands Deal and the North of Tyne CA – also reflect the need to keep Brexit within a realistic perspective:

> While Brexit is clearly the most pressing challenge
> facing the UK, it is important to recognise that
> other issues exist that both predate the 2016
> referendum and bring their own problems. Without
> Brexit, we would still have major issues to grapple
> with, such as public sector cut-backs, the reshaping
> of the benefit system, the pressures on health and
> social care, the restructuring of local government
> spending by 2020 and demographic pressures.
> Indeed, is there a danger that Brexit can serves as
> a distraction when trying to meet these challenges?
> (Cabras et al., 2017, p. 11)

Crucially, developments in the North East also herald the development of a more explicit rural dimension to local policy-making. Both in the Borderlands and North of Tyne, the new governance arrangements look forward to a much more integrated and coherent strategic approach to rural economic governance and rural productivity post-Brexit. So much so that a recent report has outlined the ambition of the region from the North of Tyne to the Scottish border to be a 'test bed for rural innovation' and captured both the challenges and opportunities for the rural north (Cowie, Mulvey, Peck, & Shaw, 2018)

There are still challenges and uncertainties. While the 'patchwork quilt' of sub-national initiatives are beginning to be stitched together in the North East, the position of the remaining NECA councils remains a problem (Shaw & Robinson, 2018) as does the lack of a wider regional framework or mechanism to allow the wider North East region (including Tees Valley) to collaborate or provide voice. There must also be the possibility that the Borderlands Deal will have to stand the test of another referendum in Scotland and the possibility of an independent Scotland applying to remain in the EU. However, as this contribution has argued, there are real grounds for hope that a more locally constituted and meaningful form of devolution will emerge from the shadow of Brexit.

7

THE NORTH EAST AS A TOURIST
DESTINATION: A HIDDEN GEM?

Tom Mordue

This chapter considers the recent development of the North East of England as a major international tourist destination, and asks: what North East are we showcasing?

INTRODUCTION

In recent times the North East of England has changed fundamentally as a place of production, built on industries such as coalmining, shipbuilding, steelmaking and engineering, to become a place of consumption as well as production. Now it not only makes and sells things, it sells itself. Those 'old' industries have largely either been lost or moved to pastures new as they responded to the forces of globalisation, economic restructuring and the perennial search for cheaper production costs. With this, the North East has had to reinvent itself as a place that draws in new industries, from high tech industries to services and tourism. Indeed, to think of the North East as a tourist destination would have been almost unthinkable only four or five decades ago. But, as Urry (2000, 2002) so famously said, everywhere and anything can be a tourist attraction in this globalised world, and even old industries like coalmining and shipbuilding and the community cultures they spawned, can become heritage attractions once they are history.

EXPLOITING HERITAGE AND CREATING ICONIC SITE ATTRACTIONS

The Beamish Open-Air Museum is an iconic example of this heritagisation of the past. Located on a large open site west of Chester le Street, its founders scoured the region in the 1960s and 1970s for artefacts from its past in order to recreate an 'authentic' early 1900s North Eastern pit village, town and open cast coalmine. All in a stage set with actors in costume to bring them alive, creating a simulacrum of the past that makes the visitor experience that much more 'real', though tamed and nostalgic. It really is an excellent place to visit, mixing education and entertainment in fine balance, which illustrates the power of tourism to turn once mundane reality into attraction. Other lived Beamish tableaux now include a 1940s farm, and a nineteenth century quilter's cottage. In development is a 1950s town as demand for visiting the region's past increases, and even recent North East history is a place to visit, not only to look at but to experience, live and walk through.

While Beamish is a marvel of its type, it is also emblematic of how we have come to manage the North East by taking much of its industrial past from the streets of the everyday, cleaning it up and putting it in a specialised 'tourist enclave' (Edensor, 2000) for convenient, safe and politically washed consumption. As for the rest of the region beyond the iconic attractions of Durham Cathedral, Castle and Palace Green; as well as Hadrian's Wall and various castles and market towns, and the like, we have shopping malls, street entertainments, festivals, fayres, spectacular football stadia and cleaned-up architecture, of which Grey Street in Newcastle upon Tyne must be the jewel in the crown. Not only this, Newcastle upon Tyne and Gateshead have taken wasteland remnants of the river Tyne's maritime and industrial past and created a waterfront playground awash with bars, restaurants, galleries, exhibition spaces, hotels and a major music venue in similar vein to what you would see in post-industrial places stretching from Liverpool to Baltimore in the United States. To a lesser extent, all the North East towns have attempted their own spatial-cultural transformations built around heritage, or at least a façade of which.

Moreover, deindustrialisation has allowed waterways to be cleaned up to the extent that the once polluted rivers such as the Tyne and the Wear offer some of the best game angling in England, and blue flags on the North East beaches are almost a matter of routine these days. The five North East universities also bring in thousands of international students each year, not to mention international academics and other visitors, which has injected a certain cosmopolitanism into the region's old, predominantly white, working-class cultural fabric. The North East region, then, has much to sell to the visitor economy, and it certainly looks better than it did, but where does the old culture fit into this postmodern regional reconfiguration?

MANAGING THE TOURIST MIRACLE

It has, of course, taken significant management to create the new (postmodern) North East; and there are numerous place-making professionals that speak to the world via a consumer language and symbolism that eschews much of the region's 'grim up North' identity. Instead, they speak of a more shiny, entrepreneurial region, signalling the North East's entry into what Robins (1991) called 'the global bazaar': the post-industrial race between places for footloose capital and people (Harvey, 1989). Indeed, besides the North East Local Enterprise Partnership that has a broad strategic economic development remit which includes tourism and culture, there are now four North Eastern destination management organisations (DMOs) covering: Hadrian's Wall, County Durham, Northumberland and Newcastle/Gateshead. Their main job is place marketing, particularly in relation to attracting tourists. However, they can have an inward investment remit too, built around the axiom that a cleaned up, attractive and cultural place is not only good for tourists, it is good for inward investment, and good for residents. Moreover, potential residents like high worth executives who might want to relocate their firms in the North East because of cheaper production values, but who might be put off by the old North East's lack of middlebrow culture (cf. Shield, 1991), including lack of an enterprise culture, are particularly prized.

THE IMPORTANCE OF THE NEWCASTLE/ GATESHEAD INITIATIVE

The Newcastle/Gateshead Initiative (NGI), the Newcastle and Gateshead DMO, is somewhat emblematic of its ilk in the way it positions the North East in these ways. Initiated in the early 2000s to drive the 2008 Newcastle/Gateshead Capital of Culture bid – which it lost somewhat controversially to Liverpool – tells us that:

> *The focus of all [NGI] activity is economic growth; the organisation works to change perceptions and*

> *create a positive profile in order to attract visitors,*
> *major conferences and events, students, new*
> *investment and jobs. (NGI website: Accessed July*
> *2019)*

It is interesting how in this statement the NGI highlights tourism's relational juxtaposition with other outside to inside priorities, signalling how tourism is indeed integral to inward investment success and connected to all those other target activities. Something which is doubly confirmed on its website as it tells us that: 'the twenty first century North East is a place of vibrancy, with a quality of life that makes it a great place to visit, live and work, study and invest', which is a strapline narrative that clearly signals how the North East is a destination: an arrival point and staging post for people and capital on the hunt for somewhere to go.

TOURISM DATA AND INDICATORS

In terms of measured successes of constructing the North East as a tourist attractor, there are indicators at hand. For example, according to a report prepared for the North East Local Enterprise Partnership's 2014 Strategic Economic Plan by This is Durham, the County Durham DMO, the North East's visitor economy generates around 3.6 billion pounds sterling of expenditure each year, which supports 54,600 jobs. Moreover, large multinational hotels and major cultural venues dot the North Eastern landscape, and transport providers, retailers and hospitality businesses, service the consumption needs of visitors in a sector in which more than 10,000 Small and Medium Enterprises now operate alongside thousands more in the supporting supply chain. It is thus not an overstatement to stress that not only is the visitor economy important both as a stand-alone sector and as an integral part of the whole North East economy, it is a major driver of social change and diversification within it.

THE NEW CULTURAL NORTH EAST

As mooted, then, it is arguable that the North East of England, like so many post-industrial regions, has undergone an identifiable postmodern cultural development phase since the 1970s (Harvey, 1989) in which tourism and a revamped cultural identity play a key, and mutually supporting, roles. Not only do discrete heritage spaces pepper the urban and rural landscape to provide soupcons of culture and 'local flavour', they do so alongside spectacular quaysides and landmarks like the Angel of the North, Middlesbrough's Bottle of Notes and the Middlesbrough Institute of Modern Art, that on the one hand celebrate the past and on the other tell us that the North East is great place, indeed a better place than it used to be, and a place that is ready to take on the future. 'Andy Capp is dead – Newcastle is alive' (Robbins, 1991) as the Intercity slogan went to herald the early days of the new North East's cultural and economic arrival. Now it has really arrived, or so its new iconic symbols tell us. But it is not just about new icons sitting alongside old ones, every corner of the region has tourist enclaves of one sort or another, which Edensor (2000) describes as places either created or sanctioned by local authorities in conjunction with powerful commercial interests and subjected to high degrees of spatial regulation. So often found in urban settings, tourist enclaves are purified spaces that, even if they in everyday urban spaces like city centres, are aesthetically and socially set apart from everyday life, where all 'undesirable elements' and social practices are likely to be deterred' (p. 328). Spontaneous social contact between locals and tourists is thus likely to be minimal in the enclave not only because of high levels of spatial regulation and surveillance but because of the array of spectacles and consumption opportunities designed to focus the 'tourist gaze' (Urry, 2000) and distracting ways. These include the usual 'global bazaar' mix of things like exotic and local street entertainments, tourist shopping, hotels, restaurants, various cultural attractions and tourist signage. A casualty is the much-vaunted North Eastern friendliness which, although heralded in regional marketing campaigns, is stilted by such arrangements because spontaneous contact between strangers is just too unpredictable for consumption focussed city centre management, and not always welcome by tourists (Wang, 2000). In these circumstances, local life can all too easily be relegated to 'local colour' and backdrop rather than providing local authenticity and uniqueness (Ritzer, 2005) to the extent that everyone is something of a stranger and passer-by in the postmodern urban centre (Mordue, 2005, 2007).

Beyond the focus of the everyday urban centre, perhaps the best recent illustration of the way the old and new North Easts coexist in current time-space is the juxtaposition of the Durham Miners' Gala (or Big Meeting) and the 2018 Great Exhibition of the North (GEOTN). Hosted by Newcastle and Gateshead as part of the Northern Powerhouse project promulgated by the Chancellor of the Exchequer 2010–2016, George Osborne, the GEOTN was a one-off event, supported by an £8 million government grant, and led by the NGI. Its purpose was to turbo-charge the North's image economy over two and a half month's period during the summer of 2018. Essentially it show-cased the North's successes in, and linkages between, art, design, innovation and enterprise, and attracted around 3.8 million visitors. Although the GEOTN was about celebrating the wider North's entrepreneurial and creative genius, the NGI took every opportunity to promote the North East in line with its strapline narrative that extolled the virtues of the North East as an exquisite place in which to do business, invest, visit, live and work as well as to:

> [...] *change people's minds about it being grim up north' and dispel the idea of the region as a place of 'flat caps and whippets'.*
> (GEOTN Chair, Gary Verity, in Tomaney, 2018a)

The Durham Miners' Gala mission is quite different, being a one-day event that has been held almost every July since it was developed by the Durham miners themselves in 1871 to celebrate their communities and their collective union as a culture and a workforce. The Gala has consistently attracted crowds of 100,000 people and many more (reportedly up to 300,000), many of whom march into Durham with colliery banners and brass bands symbolising their places, their collieries and their heritage. However, after the miners' strike of 1984–1985, collieries closed and down the country, and it appeared that not only was the mining industry dying but that working-class solidarity itself was diminishing with each pit closure. Nowhere was this felt more sharply than in the Durham coalfields as unemployment soared and their communities thrown into turmoil. As steel and shipping also exited the region, the North East economy was in deep trouble, as was its cultural identity, and the annual Durham Miners' Gala similarly went into decline, looking like an anachronism to many as attendances reduced year-on-year to the point where it seemed the decline was terminal. Then, a New Zealand entrepreneur, Michael Watt, injected much needed funds and impetus into the Gala in the 1990s, given it a more international focus as well as a local one, and it has gone from strength to strength since. In 2017, it was estimated that around 250,000 people turned up to the Gala both to celebrate mining heritage and to cheer the resurgence of a newly invigorated national Labour Party, backed by the National Miners' Union. In 2019 the event once again attracted the Leader of the Labour Party and a packed Cathedral full-house for its Mining Communities Service. It seems, then, that far from being dead, the old but current working-class culture lives on deep in the North East soul and has regrouped to move along with the new times while still being a counterpoint to them.

The contrast between the GEOTN and the Miners' Gala, then, is quite stark. The Gala is a longstanding, ongoing event that represents a self-generated cultural identity originating from an industrial past – that was originally privately owned then brought into public ownership – that fuelled the global power that was British Empire. The state in the 1980s smashed the industry by closing it down and buying cheap (subsidised) coal from abroad because it did not want to subsidise its own coal production any more or the communities that depended on it. The GEOTN, on the other hand, represents globalisation from the current demands of capital and its political economy in that it is a marketing spectacle, built from a reallocation of public funds towards the new priorities of place-making and management in order to promulgate an entrepreneurial image to attract tourists and investment. The underlying message of such a strategy seems to be that the future hangs from a cultivated, even Disneyfied, entrepreneurial culture while the past was about large industries that supplied an almost paternalistic surety even if those times were hard and grim. The old North East, then, was built from earthy collective toil, while its future is individuated, branded and clean.

CONCLUSION

Which culture does the postmodern tourist favour? According to Richards (2014), the game is up regarding spectacular attractions and the stage-managed identikit tourist honeypots that can be found just about everywhere in the usual, spatially orchestrated, manner (Mordue, 2017). Tourists want to seek out spaces beyond the tourist enclaves and cultural quarters, but more than this they want to actually 'live like a local' and exercise their 'temporary citizenship' to impact creatively on places for the good of all its citizens, not just for the benefit of capital and the middle class consumers that postmodern urban and destination management has been so fixed upon (Richards, 2014).

In this new regime of integrated consumption ... tourists and locals actively seek culturally creative, self-determined, impromptu, mutually beneficial and enjoyable experiences in real time and space. The local bar is as important as the showcase museum in this performativity as the new 'glocal' citizenry eschews top down stage management for meaningful, self-directed moments of embodied creativity and connectedness. Here (Maitland, 2013), old-fashioned friendliness and curiosity between strangers can flourish, and pop-up happenings overturn myriad local/global dualisms and rigidities that have infused the assumptions of so much urban management (Mordue, 2017).

The pop-up happenings that are most valued by current postmodern tourists, then, are not those of the GEOTN and the like, but spontaneous contact with real local people in the real place's visitors go in search of beyond the tourist pap and spectacle (also see Florida, 2002; Sacco, 2011 on cultural development). As such, advocates that tourism-related policy should shift away from the 'serial reproduction of standardised tourists' capes' in order to help areas develop in the ways that tourists and others can enjoy together. It seems the Miners' Gala fits this bill, but would its authenticity be lost by floods of tourists gathering on Durham's Racecourse to gaze at and listen to the left leaning speeches of Labour politicians and invited guests? This is doubtful because its heritage is too strong, the purpose of the meeting will not change, and because the swelled ranks of its traditional attendees on the day are once again too strong. Indeed, tourism could cement the Gala's future even further as it celebrates the old and the authentic and is prepared to pay for it. In other words, the Gala is large enough, cultural and entertaining that it would take an awful lot for tourism to denude its significance and its experiential appeal because it's always been spectacularly touristic as well as serious and celebratory.

Regarding the North East's every day (McCannell, 1973), tells us that genuinely lived authenticity is not available to tourists because of their transience, even if they are driven to seek it in the places they visit. Moreover, even if the kind of consumption-based citizenship that Richards (2014) speaks of somehow became available to tourist in the North East, authenticity available to the tourist would happen only through glimpses and happenchance. To be more consistent and predictable for the tourist, authenticity would have to come through the kind of staging provided by Beamish, for example. As for the North Easterner, living in the North East, everyday life could not tolerate the intrusion of large numbers of postmodern tourists seeking out the real and the authentic every day, therefore the staging of its culture in tourist enclaves not only sidesteps the local every day, it protects it too.

To return to the question in the chapter title: what North East are we showcasing? It is quite clear that the dominant narrative of the North East that is being showcased to the world is the one that the NGI is leading on, though the old

North East is still there on the streets and in its lived everydayness alongside that postmodern reincarnation. Is this a bad thing? Is the authentic North East being taken over by a made-over caricature and simulacrum of itself? On a pragmatic note, this is unavoidable because image is king in the race between places; and secondly, what is happening now in the North East is another chapter in the (his)story of a region that is always becoming, and never fixed. Authenticity is not simply a thing of the past either. Indeed, what is happening today is destined to become heritage once it is history. How we will celebrate that and judge it in the future is open to speculation, but one thing that we can be sure of is that, just like the past, the future of the region is a matter of politics and economics as well as culture and identity. Moreover, as we face a very uncertain European context in the coming years, the political economy of the North East region requires more skilful and visionary leadership than any cultural makeover or re-imaging strategy could ever deliver.

Tourism could be one of the sectors in the North East that does stand to benefit from Brexit, as new markets may open up internationally and especially in Asia and the United States. This has recently been explored by DCMS and the government (DCMS, 2018). However, transport infrastructure investment and the future of the East Coast rail franchise will remain critical to tourism and the future of the North East.

8

SMALL FIRMS AND INNOVATION IN THE NORTH EAST: CAN WE CREATE MORE DYNAMISM?

Michele Rusk

INTRODUCTION

The unprecedented changes in the geopolitical landscape and the metamorphoses of old party-political alignments has some dismayed and others frankly fearful. As the demise of the current political classes becomes an increasing possibility, one thing is certain, previous reality has changed and changed utterly as new political ideologies emerge. Forecasting any new dispensation and anticipating the nature of tomorrow's socio-economic realities, even soon, becomes increasing difficult. The spirit of our times is uncertain with scholars and practitioners agreeing that complex problems need more innovative, multifaceted solutions (Abbasi et al., 2019).

Now, in 2019 as the United Kingdom copes with the chaos that is Brexit, the challenges in the North East are unprecedented, unpredictable and difficult to untangle. In such circumstances, perhaps the most rational response is to equip our leaders and the next generation with the skills to respond, adapt and innovate. A growing necessity for dynamic flexibility has led to an increased focus on the effects and importance of entrepreneurship, as a way of finding direction through complexity and even embracing uncertainty. In this context, entrepreneurship is not only a driving force of economic development, structural change and job creation. It is also a way to navigate the future and address the challenge of regional development (Vyakarnam, 2009).

More people with vision are needed. Those who are energetic about change and have a passion for creating new directions, where Small and Medium Enterprises (SMEs) can thrive within an innovation ecosystem propelled by wholesale entrepreneurial ambition. It is time for a different way of leading, managing and even thinking.

THE CONTEXT

Successive governments have long put great store in entrepreneurship as a force for socio-economic good. However, Greene, Mole, and Storey (2008) looked at entrepreneurship over a 30-year period in an area of 'low' enterprise in the North East of England and concluded that 'whilst it has been a laboratory for enterprise culture experiments for 30 years, it has not resulted in any clear acceleration of entrepreneurial activity'.

Now in the UK nationally the trend is upward, with the number of business start-ups increasing and SMEs still the wellspring of innovation. Here in the North East, like anywhere else, they are the key to local economic development and job creation. This is significant when considering that almost all businesses in the North East are SMEs with 95% of these being micro-businesses or sole traders. However, since 2014 the North East has been ranked 12th out of 12 UK regions for levels of entrepreneurial aspiration (Santander Enterprise Index, 2014) and to address this the North East Local Enterprise Partnership (NELEP) plan is to create 100 thousand high skilled and higher paid private sector jobs by 2024 (NELEP, 2014).

Given these statistics the clear imperative is to inspire regional entrepreneurial ambition so as to stimulate, support and grow a vibrant and resilient small business sector with a focus on future opportunities. To this end the North East Strategic Economic Plan addresses regional economic development by targeting key areas for future focus, namely Digital, Advanced Manufacturing, Health & Life Sciences and Energy. While at the same time this strategy emphasises the fundamental potential of the service sector; specifically, Education, Financial & Business Services, Transport, Construction (NELEP, 2019b).

The real question for start-up and scale-up businesses is, not only how these new policies affect them in practice, but rather, what new and promising potential will arise from new macro-level strategic directions. In order to take full advantage of new opportunities arising from the inevitable churn that will result from Brexit, SMEs will need to become agile innovators. However, more recent research shows that while businesses see the benefit of innovation and they want to become more innovative, they just don't know how. SMEs report that they simply find innovation too challenging (27%) because of lack of time (43%) and lack of skilled staff (37%) (FSB, 2018).

THE CHALLENGE

Even without Brexit the zeitgeist is characterised by dynamic change, complexity and uncertainty with entire countries struggling to articulate their role in an amorphous geopolitical landscape. While regions grapple with new economic forms of organisation and try to anticipate the implications for social sustainability, it is no longer an option to wait for the nation to be fixed by governments alone. In these circumstances new tools are needed to manage in essentially unknowable futures. This means attending to first principles of strategic entrepreneurship leadership, altering focus and redefining where energy is directed. Entrepreneurial leaders are pivotal in this regard, as they can effect transformational change in fundamental domains such as Socio-Economic Value Creation, Global Venturing and Academic Renaissance (Rusk, 2018).

Deprived regions like the North East, need to play a leading part in shaping their own bespoke strategies for how to cope with the effects of future changes. Devising and implementing such strategies will require key regional actors to work in concert and the development of stronger self-reliance by utilising their indigenous strengths, exploiting existing international connections, leveraging intellectual property and becoming more self-financing through the creation of new circular sustainable mechanisms. Circular as opposed to linear mechanisms are a way to ensure that benefits accrue back to the original system. They achieve win–win situations by setting in motion mechanisms to induce regenerative industrial transformations that will pave the way for achieving sustainable production and consumption (Korhonena, 2018).

SMEs play a crucial role in local economies and job creation and as such they are key to regional economic buoyancy. At the national level there has been a 30% increase in the creation of SME's since 2010, but the rate SME start-up in the North East shows only a 24% increase – less than half the rate of London (53%) and way below Manchester (40%). In the North East, larger SMEs who employ 50–249, are concentrated in Manufacturing (19%), Health (13%) and Education (8%). Of those SMEs comprising one to nine people, a significant proportion are concentrated in services; professional, scientific, technical (15%), construction (12%) and retail (9%) (IPPR North, Interim Report, 2019).

Of the 99.8 % of all businesses in the North East that are SMEs, most are micro-businesses (95%) the majority of which are sole traders (74%). For these micro-businesses the challenges are considerable. It is this somewhat fragmented SME profile that may help to explain why SME productivity in the North East falls below performance nationally. Productivity in Northern SMEs, including those in the North East, lags the national average with firms of 50–99 employees 33% less productive.

The prevalence of micro-businesses and sole traders in the North East is noteworthy in terms of regional development and require a different approach to policy-making and support. In practice government support needs to harness 'grass roots' activity at the community level in order to help stimulate networking and collaborative economic initiatives. The most important consideration is to identify the strategic occasions for intervention. Such opportunities represent levers where government can act in concert with key SME sector actors to stimulate socio-economic innovation that addresses real practical issues.

KEY ENABLERS FOR SME SUCCESS

Since the twenty-first century, the emphasis has shifted from simply creating new technologies to the transformative effect of technology on society, for good and ill. Today, innovation has generally been associated with boundary crossing, collaboration and the integration of different kinds of knowledge, collectively known as knowledge transfer (NESTA, 2006). Knowledge transfer is a key element in ensuring a vibrant and sustainable SME sector especially in the wake of Brexit, because new knowledge is the source of innovation.

Notwithstanding the UK industrial Strategy aim to support universities and businesses working together to innovate. University Business Schools remain national untapped resources for economic benefit (UK Industrial Strategy, 2017.) Yet key enablers for business success have been identified as internal capacity and capability. If SMEs are to remain the wellspring of innovation clearly there is a role not only for government but also for higher education (BIS, 2013).

A JOINED-UP APPROACH

Businesses thrive in an environment that is conducive to growth, yet from the government's perspective creating entrepreneurial innovation ecosystems poses various challenges for policy-makers. Scholars and policy-makers alike have long studied the genesis of Silicon Valley in the 1950s (Adams, 2005; Hanson, 1983; Rogers & Larson, 1986). Since then the development of relationships between universities, business sectors and governments has taken different forms depending on the specific circumstances and traditions of a given city, region or country.

Etzkowitz and Leydesdorff (2000) coined the term 'Triple Helix' to describe an overlapping, series of institutional arrangements among universities, industries and the government, with hybrid organisations emerging at the interfaces. The Triple Helix analogy encompasses the specific nature of innovation that arises within each of the three institutional spheres of university, industry and government, as well as the dynamics at their intersections. The concept is a model of knowledge production and exploitation because of the relationships between all three. It brings to the fore the role for the university in stimulating the potential for innovation and economic development in a knowledge society (Erno-Kjolhed, Husted, Monsted, & Wenneberg, 2001).

A joined-up approach often only occurs in extremis when there is an overarching imperative for collaboration – it could be argued that Brexit is such a driver. For any region, but especially for a geographic area with a legacy of industrial decline, the fundamental goal is seeking prosperity and wellbeing for all its citizens. The alternative is to embark on societal crisis; prolonged and unremitting. This overarching obligation can be broken down into a trio of challenges:

- Sustainable and shared socio-economic value creation.

- International connectedness through global venturing.

- The pursuit of knowledge and transfer of knowhow in the service of self-actualisation.

Addressing these challenges requires a high degree of innovation and orchestration.

The NELEP recognises that Brexit is a complex issue with social as well as economic implications and in response has formed the North East Brexit Group made up of business representatives, the education sector, trade unions, local government and voluntary organisations. This group is focussed on the potential impact of different Brexit scenarios and related economic issues. It aims to ensure that a clear and coordinate North East voice is heard. The next step is to concentrate on ensuring that advice and support is given to North East businesses and citizens. Clearly this is about all our futures and therefore requires all available knowledge, talents and know-how to be marshalled to collectively design an imaginative, robust and workable economic development impetus (NELEP, 2019b).

GROWTH HUBS

Researchers from government and academia have forecast the potential effect of Brexit on the North East economy (NELEP, 2018a).

They predict:

- Lower levels of economic activity generally.

- A disproportionate impact because of historic reliance on automotive and pharmaceutical sectors.

- Effect on knowledge intensive services concentrated in Newcastle, Gateshead and North Tyneside.

- Heightened risks in the North East around gross domestic product and lower labour income.

Simply put this translates not to 'More and Better jobs' but to the reverse of fewer jobs, further reductions in productivity and lower wages. The situation is exacerbated by the expected demise of a whole host of Euro-Funds post-Brexit. Central government has responded and taken account of local economic conditions. It has proposed a UK Shared Prosperity Fund where individual areas should be free to allocate funding from within their allocation to projects at the pan-regional or multicounty basis (NELEP, 2018a). Crucially the consultation period on the UK Shared Prosperity Fund has been extended until after the next Spending Review or later. This delay has very significant implications for deprived regions like the North East.

Over and above financial measures, in the short- to medium-term the region plans Growth Hubs and wider business support networks to develop communications for business support and advice. But over the next three years a more coherent strategic approach will be necessary to raise the productivity of North East SMEs. The stakes are high. Were Northern SMEs, the North East included to match the national average in terms of productivity, this would achieve some £23 billion per annum and represents a 7.5% increase in Northern Gross Value Added (IPPR North, Final Report, 2019).

ENTREPRENEURIAL THINKING

Entrepreneurship is, about more than just starting a business, developing an existing one or launching a social enterprise; these define contexts for entrepreneurship in practice and approaches to learning that are inappropriately formulaic (Rusk & McGowan, 2015). Entrepreneurship must be viewed primarily as a mindset; a way of thinking that is both the catalyst and driver for developmental innovation in several different contexts. It is also insufficient to speak of the entrepreneur in such absolutist terms that suggests some people are entrepreneurs while others are not. Rather there are degrees of entrepreneurship that are often contingent on a given circumstance, the common dominator being a propensity to seek opportunities and engage in developmental innovation that can be expressed in a variety of different environments. Regardless of the context, entrepreneurship in whatever guise, whether manifest in individuals or as entrepreneurial organisations has become the driver of economic and social change and innovation, altering the future of work, the way organisations are designed, and redefining the dynamics of whole industries.

Converting ideas into innovations that make tangible new processes, products and experiences is the province of the entrepreneur; while crafting and applying insightful and timely policy has to be the work of political entrepreneurial leaders; by contrast for the academic entrepreneurial leader the task is providing opportunities for learning and generating new knowledge. These are in themselves strategic design processes. It is as a strategic designer that both industrial entrepreneurs and civic and academic entrepreneurial leaders not only create their new venture, social intervention or developmental initiative but importantly as the architects of flexibility, adaptability and ultimate sustainability. In effect such entrepreneurial individuals become orchestrators of whole innovation ecosystems that are at heart open systems networks.

These Entrepreneurial Leadership traits may be key to shaping tomorrow with the imperative to address the growing need for a fresh perspective on innovation competency development and co-creation through multifaceted entrepreneurial communities of enquiry, learning and practice. To address these complex challenges new styles of thinking at the intersection of different areas of knowledge are needed; where solutions are to be found in the multidisciplinary mix (Rusk, 2018). But the question then becomes where to look for direction?

In the face of Brexit, the North East now needs to leverage a different logic of business decision-making that, while seeking prosperity, also seeks to support the common good by reducing injustice and environmental impact. This requires local, dynamic and collaborative entrepreneurial leadership that inspires common purpose. It calls for a new approach to identifying and solving problems; spanning boundaries over a broad spectrum of disciplines; uniting values with innovative practice; and integrating corporate social responsibility with business traditions. The result would be an expansion of entrepreneurial collaborative forms to bring forth different contingency thinking and behaviours.

In practice developmental innovation is 'the stock in trade' of entrepreneurial leaders; be that through new economic ventures, new policy creation or new mechanisms of learning. However, these all take place within a context and at a juncture in time. For a post-Brexit North East, this begs the question as to how essentially local universities, government and industry can collaborate to co-create the necessary innovation mechanisms that can both ignite and sustain a unique and vibrant North East entrepreneurial ecosystem populated with a myriad of SMEs. For the challenges ahead we need entrepreneurial leaders with the vision to create shared value.

UNIVERSITY LINKS

For over a decade the UK Government has aimed to bring together universities and colleges to build a dynamic, knowledge-based economy (Innovation Nation, 2008), with policies designed to ensure that research funding encourages innovation (NESTA, October 2006). This has encouraged greater interaction between universities, the wider economy and society resulting in the emergence of entrepreneurship ecosystems. Scholars have identified several general principles that need to be followed when stimulating a culture of innovation. Policy intervention needs to take a holistic approach, focussing on the following: the entrepreneurial actors within the ecosystem; the resource providers within the ecosystem; entrepreneurial connectors within the ecosystem and the entrepreneurial environment of the ecosystem (Mason & Brown, 2014).

In addition, universities increasingly provide important regional links into the global knowledge economy (Nelson, 1993). Thus, Universities can be the catalysts for communities of practice that encompass academics, graduates, entrepreneurs and SMEs by:

- Generating knowledge needed for innovation by driving forward the research frontier while at the same time engaging in applied research to solve specific practical problems (Perkmann & Walsh, 2009).

- Providing a steady flow of well-educated graduates and environments conducive to SME start-up, such as enterprise and incubator units.

- Providing new insights of value to civil society; the public and third sectors by acting as anchors or honest brokers when collaborating with other stakeholders to co-create regional development strategies and practical innovative initiative.

KNOWLEDGE TRANSFER

The North East is home to five universities including Newcastle University and Northumbria in the City of Newcastle upon Tyne. Recent joined-up activity represents a radical new approach based on collective collaboration and co-creation and is the first step in developing an entrepreneurial laboratory for change in the North East.

Northumbria and Newcastle universities have jointly won the bid to host the 42nd annual Institute for Small Business and Entrepreneurship (ISBE) conference in 2019. The ISBE conference has a national and international reputation for the highest quality, cutting-edge entrepreneurial and small business research. ISBE's vision is to connect academic, practitioners and policy-makers to pursue excellence in small business and entrepreneurship, and the annual conference is the optimal expression of this vision. This prestigious national event is being hosted by the city of Newcastle upon Tyne in recognition of scholarly expertise in innovation, SME start-ups and entrepreneurship within higher education here.

Both universities are strongly committed to underpinning Enterprise and Innovation with impactful research that raises regional entrepreneurial aspiration. Hosting the ISBE conference will help unlock the entrepreneurial leadership ambitions within small firms in Newcastle and the North East by:

- Facilitating the regional debate on the 'Frontiers of Entrepreneurship' among practitioners, policy-makers and academics.

- Leaving a legacy of a collective interdisciplinary innovation forum to spearhead future change.

With respect to impact, Newcastle Business School at Northumbria University already plays a leading role in the region as the anchor institute to accelerate new innovative approaches to entrepreneurial leadership. Strategic Entrepreneurial Leadership (SEL) research has gained significant international attention for its cutting-edge focus on New Venturing, Civic Entrepreneurship, Responsible Entrepreneurship and Entrepreneurial Leadership by Design.

SEL is contributing to the international academic debate through new theoretical modelling of entrepreneurship which articulates the principles of developmental innovation through a Strategic Design Dynamics framework that sets out:

- Entrepreneurial leadership as the catalytic principle.

- Strategic design as the animating principle.

- Open innovation as the navigating principle.

SEL research findings clarify the essential characteristic of entrepreneurial leaders as their ability to create shared value through developmental innovation in the socio-economic domain. Consequently, a new design dynamics model has been developed as a scaffold upon which to shape regional innovation ecosystems. This research and innovation activity also underpins practical SME engagement and facilitates better understanding of the nature of entrepreneurial leadership, its role in stimulating regional innovation ecosystems and how to build capacity in the North East.

In addition, Newcastle Business School has pioneered accessible and practical business support by matching university expertise across all business disciples with SME needs through a ground-breaking Business Clinic. This model helps SMEs in the North East to increase productivity by engaging with university staff and students to access pro-bono business consultancy, which provides the latest knowledge from a range of disciplines, leading to positive business outcomes.

The Business Clinic has identified substantial demand for advice on digitisation and internationalisation across a range of SMEs in the North East. It is currently conducting further research into the barriers restricting SME performance, in consultation with the NELEP, Regional Technology Centre and North East Chamber of Commerce. The Business Clinic model is a straightforward, bottom-up method for universities to support SMEs scale-up across the region. Currently preparations are underway to expand the Business Clinic model out across the country.

FUTURE SKILLS

Skills shortages are more acute for SMEs than for large businesses. In 2017, almost one-third of vacancies in firms with fewer than five employees were 'hard to fill' because of difficulties in finding suitably skilled candidates; this compares to just 16% in firms with 250 or more employees (IPPR North, Final Report, 2019)

Adaptability in organisations, individuals and society will become ever more essential for navigating the changes ahead. The key skills anticipated are problem-solving, adaptability, collaboration and leadership. In order to thrive, SMEs will need pivotal people who can create and add fundamental value. There will also be a need the more human skills of creativity, innovation, imagination and design especially in a more automated existence.

In future everyone; organisations, SMEs and individuals alike, will need to adapt to economic and political change and be willing to acquire new skills and experiences in order to be prepared for fundamental systemic shifts not only in the world of work but also in the society, in general. In these circumstances the core skills are of leadership, creativity and innovation are essential (PWC, 2018).

CONCLUSIONS

It may no longer be possible to plan future strategies effectively, given the changing nature of the economy and the political landscape. The fundamental challenge that Rosabeth Moss Kanter (1997) called for over 20 years ago still remains 'how to equip future leaders with the imagination to innovate, the professionalism to perform, and the openness to collaborate: leading to change-adept organisations and systems'.

For SMEs in the North East to flourish, a wholesale environmental shift that focusses on 'a rising tide raising all ships' needs to occur. This is nothing short of the creation of a better vision to raise entrepreneurial ambition and means every stakeholder, from local government, industry and academia, working more together to develop a more systemic innovation culture for the region. If it is to remain relevant and take advantage of the considerable opportunities the new dispensation of a post-Brexit world will hold.

Consequently, it is now timely to examine the potential for marshalling collective intelligence, creativity, resources and indigenous strengths to raise entrepreneurial ambition across the board.

If Brexit is not the catalyst, what is?

PART III

NEW STRATEGIES FOR PUBLIC SECTOR CHANGE: CROSSING BOUNDARIES

9

'WHOSE BUSINESS GROWTH HUB IS IT ANYWAY?' CO-PRODUCTION OF A NEW APPROACH TO BUSINESS SUPPORT FOR THE NORTH EAST OF ENGLAND

Rob Wilson, Mike Martin and David Jamieson

INTRODUCTION

This chapter briefly outlines the literature relating to business support, presents a case study which explores the initial response of a Local Enterprise Partnerships (LEP) to the challenge of providing a 'Business Growth' hub. It then reports on a project the authors were engaged in which applied co-production approach to a sociotechnical system framing approach to development and change of a 'Growth Hub' and suggesting that Higher Education Institutions (HEIs) have a key part to play in the shaping of Small and Medium

Enterprise (SME) support programmes to meet the challenges of a post-BREXIT business environment.

The challenge to be addressed concerned the engagement of a core set of stakeholders in a co-production process, with a local LEP and other stakeholders, to work with the 'installed base' of business support activities in a region of northern England. The approach we adopted supports long-term planning based on the interests of the members of the wider network, rather than on the often narrow prescriptive, understandings and interests of policy-makers or of the organisations enacting programmes. The proposed model seeks to contribute to the current debate on the role of HEIs in strengthening regional economic development and business support by enabling and facilitating changes in the role of the supported businesses from that of mere customers and recipients to potential co-producers of advice and services, based on shared vision and a common infrastructure.

A 'RECENT' HISTORY OF BUSINESS SUPPORT

Business Support Programmes involve the combined efforts between national and local government, industry, universities professionals and businesses in interventions intended to contribute to the growth and economic development of a region. Literature about Business Support is heterogeneous due to the variety of programmes that have been developed and implemented as well as the range institutions promoting and delivering them (Mole & Bramley, 2006; Mole, Hart, Roper, & Saal, 2009; Storey, 2003). While the most representative term used to study these programmes is 'Business Support' (Sivaev, 2013) other terms, such as Local Economic Initiatives (Eisenschitz & Gough, 1998) have been used. The identification of the terms and the field helps to provide a theoretical framework to understand and analyse the different initiatives proposed for business support, as well as to propose new alternatives to the current programmes. Much research has described and evaluated the type of activities traditionally offered to SMEs through these programmes. Business support services traditionally consist of a variety of financial aids, information and signposting services, training support and practical planning advice. In addition, the Business Support programmes have included training and development of skills identified as important to the existing large industries of a region or as strategic factors for future development (Curran, 2000; Cumming & Fischer, 2012; Mole et al., 2006; Storey, 2003).

Founded in 1992 Business Support programmes, in England, were promoted, by different governments, under the broad banner of Business Link (Bennett, 2008; Curran, 2000). Latterly, these were organised regionally in their final form based on the nine areas of the Regional Development Agency's (RDAs). The approach culminated in the Information, Diagnostic, Brokerage and Transaction model under the auspices of RDAs. The implementation of the Business Link programmes followed a more or less consistently top-down approach (Bennett, 2008; Mole & Bramley, 2006; Mole et al., 2009). A key part of the activity was the provision of information and signposting services. This included information necessary to identify and access a range of resources such as companies with similar or complimentary interests, prospective partners, supply chain members or providers of support services, as well as information about the range of programmes and aids provided by public and private institutions. Practical assistance often includes a higher level of engagement and longer-term involvement such as business incubation, the preparation of applications for grants or the development and facilitation of export plans and initiatives.

One of the success factors that has been identified in such programmes is associated with the activities of cohorts of business advisors (Curran, 2000; Mole, 2002). However, the dependence of the programmes on the skills of advisors was proven to be a risky strategy, given the mobility of these employees and the corresponding risk associated with continuity of funding, which traditionally comes from government, limiting the life span of these programmes to the budget timeframes and success criteria assigned by the sponsors. The perceived efficacy and trustworthiness of the relationship between business advisors and their clients has been shown to be sensitive to continuity and their specific nature; accountants and bank managers, for example, are seen as trusted brokers to support and sources of advice. These considerations resulted in a preference for a more infrastructural and longer-term personalised approach in the approach to business support be adopted rather than more simple generic approaches, but the precise detail and implications of this remain unclear (Cumming & Fischer, 2012; Mole et al., 2009; Mole, Hart, Roper, & Saal, 2011; Storey, 2003).

After the change of Government and the formation of the Coalition in 2010, there was a short gap when the entire future of business support service was in significant doubt. This was partially due to the scepticism about the efficacy of the current programme of Business Support outlined in Richard Report to the Conservative Party Shadow Cabinet (Richard, 2008). Of which a significant part was subsequently implemented by the government department of Business Innovation and Skills under the *Local Growth* agenda (BIS, 2010). The new policy and approach involved disbanding the RDAs and regional Business Links in 2011. Business Support services were delivered via a national website and call centre until 2012, and this transitioned into a section of the wider Gov.uk site (Mole, Hart, & Roper, 2014). The regional Government Office's and RDA's were partially replaced in 2012 by LEPs in England (albeit on a different geographical footprint) with three areas of strategic activity being defined as the initial priorities for LEPs programmes of development and support: these were Skills, Training and Labour Market support, the sponsorship of Innovation networks and the creation and implementation of a new programme for Business Support in the wider context of regional Smart Specialisms (usually based on established business sectors in a LEP area). This was conducted under the banner of 'Business Growth' which sought to target resources on SMEs with ambitions to expand their operations. Across the development of the LEPs, there seems to have been an element of constructive ambiguity in the articulation of policy resulting in both national level and local explorations and discussions about the approach to be taken. It is in the context of the exploration of what a 'Business Growth' hub could mean and how it could be procured, by stakeholders and interested parties, that the work we now describe took place.

THE METHODOLOGY OF CO-PRODUCTION

The notion of co-production is rooted in the work of Ostrom and Baugh (1973) who developed the concepts in the context of seemingly intractable breakdown of community–police relations. After a long hiatus, the approach has become popularised mostly in the context of developing new approaches to services for, and with, those with complex needs (Brandsen, Verschuere, & Steen, 2018).

Co-production has been defined as the 'joint production of public services between citizens and state' (Mitlin, 2008). Pestoff and Brandsen (2007) identify three dimensions or levels of co-production – co-production with service users, co-management with user groups and co-governance. For us this expands the canvas of co-production as a means of bridging the conversation between 'stakeholders' in the process of designing and enacting sociotechnical responses to the challenges of implementing policy programmes (McLoughlin & Wilson, 2013; Wilson, Maniatopoulos, Martin, & McLoughlin, 2012) in this case the context of 'Business Support'. Engaging explicitly in bridging or 'boundary spanning' processes (Aldrich & Herker, 1977) with policy and practice communities is an essential role for Universities in response to an environment where the sector are increasingly challenged to account for their wider contribution to the economy. For instance, the 'Impact Case studies' in the Research Excellence Framework exercise of 2014 and the newly proposed Knowledge Exchange Framework. The Newcastle Business School at Northumbria University is highly successful in these terms recently achieving the accolade of Business School of the year, holder of the Small Business Charter and the work of Business Clinic (where SMEs work with students on consultancy projects). This study situates the role of the HEIs beyond these orthodox 'boundary spanning' work of specific academic entrepreneurship, research, consultancy and continuing professional development provision and proposes a space for innovative form of activity in the mode of 'boundary-shaking' of the existing assumptions and relationships of a system (Balogun, Gleadle, Hailey, & Willmott, 2005).

In the case of the work being discussed here (2013–2014) the research team adopted a co-production process with the representatives of the LEP to work with the wider 'ecology' or 'installed base' of business support networks and activities in a northern region of England. Specifically, it was aimed at engaging the stakeholders in an approach which supports long-term planning based on the interests of the members of the network, rather than on often narrow prescriptive interests of the policy-makers or the organisations enacting such programmes (Wilson et al., 2012). This was initiated with the specific aim of working in collaboration to shape a future (based on a sociotechnical architecture including complimentary collaborative and technical elements – see Cherns, 1987; McLoughlin & Wilson, 2013) which would potentially outlast the current generation of LEP structures (which in England at that point appeared relatively unpredictable). This study was conducted through a series of co-production workshops with engagement initially scoping views from a range of public and private sector stakeholders (including businesses, businesses providing support services and business networks) of the challenges of business support. This was followed analysis of the findings to inform the second stage of work with the representatives of the LEP and stakeholders to co-produce a high level or reference architecture (RA) of a local Growth Hub for a subsequent procurement.

OUR FINDINGS

An initial workshop/focus Group event, involving 40 or so participants in a loosely guided discussion, explored the concept and experience of Business Support Services. It revealed that the concept of Business Support was contended among the different stakeholders both in terms of what counted as support, which channels of support/advice were useful and appropriate and what constituted a high quality experience. Unsurprisingly, perhaps some of those providing private sector services argued that 'people only value information if they pay for it' from trusted sources. Whereas others maintained that government could be the only point of 'truth' about certain legislation and schemes to incentivise innovation or encourage the growth of businesses albeit in a context where many stakeholders felt the situation was unstable and 'always changing'. Networks of peers and professionals were valued as they were more likely to understand the problem and local contexts and individual businesses had varied experiences and found their previous encounters with the state supported Business Link service both helpful and unhelpful in equal measure.

The role of Digital channels was widely accepted to be pervasive and a key element in finding information although there was a common issue of there being 'too much information – disorganised and without clear quality'. Digital was also key to maintenance of relationships particularly for those running dedicated business networks but stakeholders remained sceptical about the potential of automation without significant investments in 'form filling' which in their experience rarely profiled businesses in useful ways rather it being for the benefit ('meeting KPIs') of those collecting the information.

It became clear in these and subsequent discussions about the future of Business Support that there was a wide range of conflicting opinions, a high level of scepticism and mistrust, particularly about continuity, specificity and neutrality of a service in particular the context of Government sponsored business information and support services. Much of the rhetoric was negative and this had been exacerbated by the decision to shift the channel to an almost exclusively online means of delivery. One typical response to the digital channel approach that had been adopted by the LEP was 'Not another ******* web site!'.

We held a subsequent workshop, with a smaller number of participants, half of whom had attended the previous discussion, and all of whom were seen in the LEP area to have some role or stake in the procurement of a 'Business Growth Hub'. In this session we adopted the strategy of encouraging the exposure of the paradox and scepticism which pervades the lived experience and literature (both policy and academic) about business support and which characterised our first session. By signalling that criticism and doubt were admissible, we were able to validate the analysis that we had made of the current situation and surface the various positions in the room. In order to move the co-production process forward, we concluded this first part of the session, with some carefully selected rhetoric which was designed to be useful and positive intervention, providing a vocabulary of terms that, if adapted and adopted, could move the discussion forward in a constructive way. The first example of this involved exhibiting the headings: 'Sustainable Diversity, Dependable Governance, Effective Curation' which was a direct response to the problems outlined in the first workshop. We then invited the participants to discuss what these terms could mean in the context we were discussing. These were then further elaborated, again as the triggers for discussion rather than the assertions of a presentation, which included:

- A safe space for encounter, discovery, conversation and transactions.

- Actors can be reliably recognised or be appropriately anonymous.

- All content has a clear provenance.

- There is a clear and trusted point of recourse.

The response to these provocations from the participating stakeholders varied ranging from those who engaged in collaborative debate opened up by this shift in rhetoric and terminology while some remained sceptical wedded to their prevailing views about the ways and means of delivering business support.

In the second part of the workshop session we iteratively built a model which we called a 'Reference Architecture', explaining this concept as a vision of where we may be going as our longer-term target (see Fig. 9.1). The model

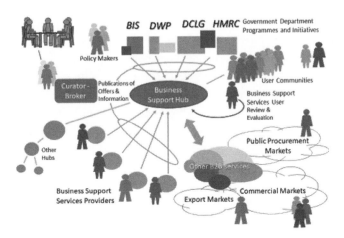

Fig. 9.1. Business Growth Hub: Proposed 'Reference Architecture'.

itself represents the 'Growth Hub' at the centre, neither as an exclusively 'digital' or 'analogue' space of engagement. The 'Hub' is represented instead as a publication and service transaction space with the intention of foregrounding a sociotechnical perspective (McLoughlin & Wilson, 2013). Taking this approach, which explicitly recognises the inherently distributed and multi-agency character of an endeavour such as business support, scaffolded the potential for an enriched deliberative occasion (which in this case moved the debate beyond the usual arguments about the provision and nature of business support services).

At the top of the RA model it included the channel(s) to central government services from different departments, which was seen the main purpose of the 'Growth Hubs' as seen from the Central Government perspective, namely as a platform for dissemination and uptake of initiatives. We also represented local services (business support providers), users and user communities. The diagram also signifies the relationship between the hub and the service it offers and the wider world of other 'Growth Hubs', B2B services, commercial home and export markets and to the public sector and its procurements.

The iconography of the 'Reference Architecture' figure is carefully selected to provoke observations and questions, such as 'Who is that?' and 'I'm one of those!'. Particular attention was paid in the discussion to the questions "Who are 'those' people, the curators and brokers?" 'Who are the governors of this hub and who might they be in the long term?' 'Should we be attempting to make an investment that will outlive the current programme and policy to create some longer lasting infrastructure?' Finally, there remained the question of the relationship between our hub and the hubs of other LEPs: with questions posed such 'Did we have anything to offer them?' 'Were we interested in any of their offers?'

A version of 'Reference Architecture', and an overview of the questions and issues it raised, was subsequently included in the 'Growth Hub' procurement documentation and impacted on the language of the LEP and the potential providers who demonstrated their level of engagement by the attempts to respond by positioning their bids in relation to the architecture. Latterly, it also had impact on the strategic thinking within the LEP about the relationships between the Business Growth initiatives and to other strands of the portfolio regarding skills, innovation and a regional observatory. Unfortunately, perhaps the vision, which emerged from the co-production process, which required the emergence of the 'Growth hub' as an infrastructural community asset operating under a collective governance model has yet to be achieved. This was perhaps inevitable in the context of the continued centralised control and sporadic funding of the 'Growth hubs' which emphasise short-term tactical achievements and measurements (such as the number of businesses registered to the hub). The key aim for exploiting the 'hub' was the adoption of a longer-term strategy aimed at generating sustainable public value via targeted engagements aimed at supporting the existing critical mass of users working with the 'installed base' of business community networks in the region.

CONCLUSIONS

This chapter reports on a process which applied a systemic framing of the problem by utilising a co-production approach to change to long-standing issues in the government support of business organisations. The intervention approach that is described makes a contribution to the current debates on business support by proposing a conceptual change in thinking of the role of the businesses from mere recipients (customers) of services to potential co-producers within a wider network of communities (of both place and interest) hosted on a sociotechnical infrastructure. To succeed such a vision needs to be underpinned by a movement towards a shared vision of infrastructure for the delivery of business support which enables heterogeneous agents and institutions to contribute to governable and sustainable progress.

The co-production approach applied in this case has the added benefit of moving beyond reductive notions of 'what works' or 'making changes because we must show we differentiate from the previous policy' by providing a lens by which to focus on the sociotechnical infrastructural and human/social capital aspects of such a hub. This opens up spaces for further co-production discussions to enhance the possibility of reuse and repurposing in the face of changing policies and economic conditions highly likely in a post-BREXIT context. Thus, it requires the flexibilities to develop regions and localities capacity to collaborate with the agents and institutions involved. This in turn supports the need for local differentiation and meaningful participation in a long-term local governance process for the ongoing innovation of relationships (Wilson et al., 2012) in order to meet diverse business and community needs rather than merely responding to the inevitability of sporadic investment in overly generic programmes initiated by national government.

With the impending changes that BREXIT will bring beyond 2020 we are in a context where business support programmes will be subject to significant pressures as the challenges and opportunities of a new environment emerge. With many business support programmes coming to a conclusion as European funding is withdrawn, new approaches are needed to reflect on what business support is, what is needed, how stakeholders will work together and apply their learning to the production of new programmes which will come on stream after 2020. We along with the other authors in this book would strongly advocate for the Public and University sector in the North to co-operate in shaping these programmes as commissioners, participants and providers to meet the challenges ahead. Equally important from our work is the mutual engagement in the cultivation of the supporting ecosystems for 'joining-up' (in this case a 'Business Growth hub') through the sort of 'boundary-shaking' co-production outlined here. HEIs are in a unique position to provoke, challenge and unleash the sort of creative thinking between stakeholders, which the BREXIT situation demands, in order to make sense of, re-shape and respond to the changing dynamics of local and regional economies particularly in a part of the UK that relies heavily on trade with the EU. In parallel to also work on the information infrastructures for addressing multi-agency challenges, such as business support, on which resources which promote sustainable diversity, dependable governance and effective curation are essential (McLoughlin & Wilson, 2013).

10

DEVELOPING PUBLIC SECTOR ENTREPRENEURSHIP IN THE UNIVERSITIES: ACCELERATING INNOVATION IN THE NORTH

James A. Cunningham

INTRODUCTION

Universities are now seen as contributors to economic, social, technological and wealth creation of the regions they inhabit through their teaching, research and technology and knowledge transfer activities (see Cunningham, Guerrero, & Urbano, 2017). Increasingly, universities are putting in place formal organisational structures and programmes that enhance and build their collaborations with industry, public sector and non-for-profit organisations. This can range from designing and running degree apprenticeship programmes for organisations or industry sectors to supporting student, graduate and faculty entrepreneurship through incubators, accelerators and business plan competitions. Within universities there has been a change in how they support entrepreneurship and innovation inside and outside their university communities. Consequently, there is a rise of entrepreneurial universities as Guerrero et al. (2014, p. 434) notes:

> *university authorities need to recognize their core role at this time as not only building but also enforcing the university entrepreneurship ecosystem that nurtures entrepreneurial potential (incentives, new learning tools, role models) as well as stimulating skills, competences and tools that are most useful, creating entrepreneurial mindsets that drive innovation (not only inside universities but also within the existent firms) and becoming entrepreneurial organizations.*

UK entrepreneurial universities do have an economic impact with more research-intensive universities have this highest economic impact with respect to entrepreneurial spin-off (see Guerrero, Cunningham, & Urbano, 2015). Moreover, businesses benefit by having close collaborations with universities such as through access to new knowledge, lower R&D costs and those firms with university collaborations are more innovative (Cunningham & Link, 2015; George, Zahra, & Wood, 2002; Lee, 2000).

Through public sector entrepreneurship programmes governments design funding programmes that are designed to enhance university industry collaborations and to support the creation of knowledge. Link and Leyden (2015, p. 14) define public sector entrepreneurship as

> *innovative public policy initiatives that generate economic prosperity by transforming a status-quo economic environment into one that is more conducive to economic units engaging in creative*

> *activities in the face of uncertainty. Through policy*
> *initiatives that are characterized by public sector*
> *entrepreneurship, there will be more development*
> *of new technology and hence more innovation*
> *throughout the economy.*

Hayter, Link, and Scott (2018) argue that there is a need for governments to purse more public sector entrepreneurship programmes. In the UK the Knowledge Transfer Partnership programmes that are designed to support university industry collaborations and have a direct benefit on the industry partner (Gertner et al., 2011). The UK Government's current Industrial Strategy could be viewed as a wide range public sector entrepreneurship programme that is reflective of the definition posited by Link and Leyden (2015). In her book *The Entrepreneurial State: Debunking Public VS Private Sector Myths*, Mazzucato (2015) argues that the origins of scientific knowledge that we experience in our daily lives come from public investment in science or what she termed as 'mission orientated science'. Mazzucato (2015, p. 6) notes

> *in countries that owe their growth to innovation –*
> *and in regions within those countries, like Silicon*
> *Valley – the State has historically served not just*
> *as an administrator and regulator of the wealth*
> *creation process, by a key actor in it and often*
> *a more darling one, will to take the risks that*
> *businesses won't.*

Consequently, these perspectives would suggest that the public sector entrepreneurship does have a significant and lasting influence on society and on long-term economic prospects. In essence, such public sector entrepreneurship does matter and can influence how different regions within the UK can sustain themselves economically and socially.

The North East has five universities within the region. They are serving the needs and demands of their stakeholders in different ways while all competing in a more globalised education market. North East universities account for 3% of the total of UK universities and they cater for 100,300 students in 2015/16 (see HESA, 2017), with 10,735 being international first year students. The more recent assessment of the economic impact of UK universities shows that they account for 1.3% of all UK employment, account for 2.9% of GDP and investment in universities have greater returns than spending on health and defence (see Universities UK, 2017a). Taking the North East, international students net economic contribution to the region in 2015/16 was estimated as £0.98 billion (see HEPI, 2018). The last economic impact assessment of higher education in the North East found that the combined impact to regional gross value added (GVA) is £1.6 billion, accounts for 2.8% of the workforce in the region and attracted 40,505 students from other parts of the UK to take up studies in the region (UK Universities, 2014). Moreover, in the last 10 years according to the NELEP (2018b, p. 10) annual economic outlook the region secured £165.3 million from UK Research Councils with the top five subject areas being energy, ICT, astronomy-observation, civil engineering and built environment and material sciences and 4.5% of the employment in the region are in the areas of science, engineering and technology professional roles.

Since the Brexit referendum UK universities have adopted different measures to offset and mitigate short-, medium- and long-term effects. This has included such initiatives setting up European campuses such as Northumbria University in Amsterdam, establishing institution-to-institution strategic partnerships such as Imperial and TU Munich. At more informal levels institutions and academics continue their international engagements to reassure international partners of their long-term commitment and intent to maintain and build upon established relationships. In addition, many UK universities have reaffirmed their support for EU students and faculty. Along with regular updates and information they have set up specific tangible initiatives to demonstrate their support and solidarity. On a more system wide perspective UK Universities along with Academy of Medical Sciences, the British Academy, the Royal Society and other key national institutions have stated that government to spend at least 2.4% of GDP on publicly funded research and development which is currently 0.76% below the 2017 GDP expenditure.[1]

CHALLENGES FACING THE ENTREPRENEURIAL UNIVERSITY

International comparison studies or what are more commonly known as international league tables affirms the international standing, reputation, performance and global outlook of UK universities. There is intense competition between universities to attract home and international students and for research funding (Dill, 2007; Geuna & Martin, 2003; Hoare, 1991). The effect of the EU referendum result like other sectors has added further uncertainties and challenges to the university sector, particularly as how best to position the sector over the short- to medium-term to meet the significant economic and social challenges that will arise irrespective of the modality of exit from the European Union. Added to this, UK universities are facing more broader macro-environmental drivers that are influencing entrepreneurial universities and those seeking to exploit their scientific discoveries through innovation and entrepreneurship. First, there is an increasing expectation by policy-makers and industry that universities are more actively involved in supporting innovation and entrepreneurship within the locality in which they inhabit. Therefore, entrepreneurial universities are becoming an integral stakeholder in regional entrepreneurial ecosystems (see Cunningham, Lehmann, Menter, & Seitz, 2019). Second, open science and open innovation are changing the way in which scientific discoveries are being exploited by firms across an array of industries. Open science is moving towards making publicly funded science more available (see Hesse, 2018; Woelfle, Olliaro, & Todd, 2011), and open innovation, is opening the array of outside partners that firms collaborate with in exploring and exploiting knowledge for innovation purposes. These drivers are fundamentally changing firm level innovation management, business models and creating new market opportunities that can be exploited on more collaborative basis. Third, public sector entrepreneurship programmes nationally and internationally are adopting mission orientated characteristics in their programme design such as requiring more industry and or third sector partners, more interdisciplinary and having clear and realistic implementable commercialisation and knowledge transfer plans. This in turn is putting different pressures on scientists in the principal investigator role leading such large-scale public research programmes (see O'Kane, Zhang, Cunningham, & O'Reilly, 2017; O'Kane, Zhang, Daellenbach, & Davenport, 2019). It is also leading to potentially different types of academic entrepreneurs and entrepreneurial academics in entrepreneurial universities and public research organisations (Miller, Alexander, Cunningham, & Albats, 2018). Fourth, who funds science and scientific discoveries – Government or industry? Increasingly many public sector entrepreneurship programmes are now being designed in such a way that it requires industry partners to co-fund research programmes.

At an institutional level entrepreneurial UK university are facing more specific drivers that coupled with Brexit provide a challenging environmental context to operate in. First, is the need to diversity their income business models away from an over reliance on student fees. The Augar Report as it more commonly known recommended changes to student fees charged by universities, reform and resources made available to further education colleges and have greater flexibility with respect to lifelong learning. Second, in responding to the increasing economic imperative entrepreneurial universities need to plan and implement what formal institutional arrangements that they are going to invest in to support entrepreneurship and innovation within and outside their universities communities (see Dolan, Cunningham, Menter, & McGregor, 2019). The final driver has been the change academic work (see Clark, 1983, 1989) where teaching, research and administration as just some aspects of the wider portfolio of activities that academic are expected to undertake. In a UK context different rounds of national research evaluations (RAE/REF) have been studied in terms of individual and institutional impacts (see MacDonald, 2017; Sayer, 2014; Schäfer, 2016) and new evaluation systems are coming into situ including a Teaching Excellent Framework (see Wild & Berger, 2016) and Knowledge Excellence Framework[2] which is being led by Research England. Like REF these evaluation frameworks will in time shape individual academic lives, influence decision-making along and investments of UK universities.

For those charged with policy-making in the domains of education, science and technology the main driving challenge remains how to maximise the return on investment in public science for the British economy and society. These policy domains and the policies that are adopted by Government does influence regional economies and societies. The overarching government policy in this domain The Industrial Strategy has articulated five foundations of ideas, people, infrastructure, business environment and place. The core challenge in delivering such an ambitious policy programme is ensuring coherency and complimentary within and among different policy strands.

SUSTAINING AND ACCELERATING INNOVATION
AND ENTREPRENEURSHIP

Through membership of the EU UK researchers can participate in a variety of EU funding schemes and UK entrepreneurs
receive support through EU structural funding mechanism
such as the ERDF programme. UK universities have been able
to build a large network of European institutional collaborations particularly through the Erasmus that have benefited their
students and have enhanced the internationalisation of their
programmes at undergraduate level. In relation to the higher
education sector the House of Commons (2019d, p. 9) noted:

> *The EU has very limited competence in the area of*
> *education policy; in particular, the provision and*
> *regulation of the HE sector (including access to*
> *student finance) is a matter for Member States.*

Irrespective of the modalities of exit, in a post-Brexit scenario
a key challenge is sustaining and accelerating national innovation and entrepreneurship at a level that maintains and grows
the UK economy and that benefits its society. This will be challenging to achieve given other significant demands that will be
placed on public expenditure. So how should the universities in
the North East contribute to sustaining and accelerating innovation and entrepreneurship that benefits the region?

First, are the North East universities should continue their
trajectory of focussing on academic excellence and quality. This
requires a sustained and consistent investment in the student
experience, lifelong learning programmes and investing people,
facilities and infrastructure. In short, they must become entrepreneurial organisations as Guerrero et al. (2015) suggest. Second, is maintaining and growing academic mobility to ensure
the region can attract the best academic and student talent
that propels new knowledge creation and scientific discovery.

Third, is universities should focus on strengthening existing local partnerships and networks, as well as European based ones, that benefits their academic communities but also their partners in the North East region. Fourth, is supporting capacity and resilience building of communities and localities in the region. This might range from sharing of expertise to being actively involved in supporting social enterprises and community groups. This also encompasses collaborating with public agencies in supporting them in their innovation and corporate entrepreneurship endeavours. Universities while growing their international focus and footprint, they also need to embed themselves more deeply within the localities they inhabit. Lastly, is building university industry collaborations and entrepreneurial university architectures that meet the needs of industry, entrepreneurs, innovators and students inside and outside the region. Universities in the region are building their university industry collaboration through developing strategic partnerships with key sectors and employers in the region that covers research and programme provisions to meet current and future needs. Also, universities continue through entrepreneurial university architectures provide incubators, accelerators, business plan competitions, knowledge transfer activities, etc., which are designed to meet the needs of nascent student, faculty and external nascent entrepreneurs. The pace of such activities should be accelerated further so the North East does not lag other UK regions.

CONCLUDING THOUGHTS

The North East has been well served well by its universities over the decades that have contributed to the vibrancy and attractiveness of the region. Brexit provides clear challenges for its universities who are already addressing and attempting to meet a myriad of demands and expectations placed on them by various stakeholders. The region needs universities to meaningfully support how the region copes with the effects of Brexit and thrives in an environment where the UK is no longer a member of the EU. Universities and their academic communities – student, faculty and profession services – can provide underpinning human capital development, infrastructure, international linkages and access to new knowledge through research that will be necessary to sustain and contribute to the growth of the economic and social vibrancy of the region over the next decade. Therefore, our regional universities need to ensure they have the appropriate structures, capabilities and capacity to secure resources from public sector programmes to support the ongoing development of the region. Moreover, our regional universities have an important economic and societal role to support the region irrespective of the final arrangements that are made between the UK and EU. They can also contribute to the forging of a regional ambition that builds on its established strengths and also ensures the region has the strategic posture to cope with the many challenges it will face beyond Brexit from other some systemic changes due to disruptive technologies, climate change and changing in the nature of work. In essence, to support the acceleration of regional innovation and entrepreneurship through participation in public sector entrepreneurship programmes, our regional universities need to nurture entrepreneurial potential throughout the region and enhance their own entrepreneurialism to effective respond to the challenges and opportunities that lie ahead for the region.

NOTES

1. See https://www.universitiesuk.ac.uk/news/Pages/Research-and-innovation-key-to-plans-for-UK-prosperity.aspx
2. https://re.ukri.org/knowledge-exchange/knowledge-exchange-framework/

11

RESEARCH, KNOWLEDGE EXCHANGE AND IMPACT: THE EXPERIENCE OF A UNIVERSITY–PUBLIC SECTOR PARTNERSHIP IN NORTH EAST ENGLAND

John Mawson and Martyn Griffin

INTRODUCTION

This chapter sets out the experience of a University–Public Sector Partnership engaged in research, knowledge exchange and impact operating across the North East England in the period from 2009 to 2019. The Institute for Local Governance (ILG) was established to facilitate research collaboration between some of the region's major public sector institutions and its academic community. The partnership emerged from a three-year period of dialogue between the regional representative bodies concerning the best way to access and utilise University research in the sphere of local public sector policy and management. The ILG was launched at the point when the consequences of the international financial crisis and the onset of policies of austerity were beginning to impact on the public sector in the North East. Throughout the past decade, the development of the ILG has been recorded, monitored and evaluated by independent consultancy support on behalf of the partnership. This work has been paralleled by research funded by the ESRC Venture Scheme undertaken by the ILG team involving interviews of participants and case studies, which is ongoing.

Against this background, the chapter sets out the rationale for the ILG, its modus operandi, research outputs and the role played by Northumbria University as an example of the involvement of one of the region's five Universities.

BACKGROUND – THE KNOWLEDGE INTERMEDIARY

The role of the ILG acting at the interface between research and practice is sometimes referred to as a knowledge broker or a knowledge exchange 'intermediary' vehicle, the nature of which is becoming more prominent in UK research policy and practice (Knight & Lyall, 2013; May, Perry, Hodson, & Marvin, 2009; Williams, 2002). The approach seeks to build a bridge between research and policy communities, facilitating their interaction so that they are better able to understand each other's goals, activities and institutional cultures. In particular, it has sought to forge ongoing working relationships with academics and practitioners in the development and use of knowledge and research in the world of practice (Mawson, 2009a; Mawson, 2009b).

In the case of the ILG Partnership, it has focussed on the field of regional and local governance within a geographical sphere of operational activity stretching from the Scottish Borders to North Yorkshire. This Partnership has comprised

Police, Fire and Rescue Services, single tier county councils and unitary local authorities within the urban areas of Teesside and Tyne and Wear. Its work has involved facilitating best practice and innovative solutions to a wide and increasingly complex range of public policy issues, often involving research on interagency working and engagement with the private sector, community and third sector bodies.

The contemporary trends in sub-national politics, public administration and public policy together with mounting regional inequalities and the impact on disadvantaged individuals and communities, raises many important research questions in which the insights of academics working together with public sector practitioners can make a significant contribution.

In the case of local government, for example, many key elements of the traditional and multipurpose municipal role have been removed by successive post-war governments. In recent years this has been referred to as the 'hollowing out' of the local state alongside the application of so-called 'new public management' techniques and approaches (Leach, Stewart, & Jones, 2018). Alongside a declining resource base, local government has been forced to retract from various statutory and non-statutory services in areas such as economic development, youth facilities, parks and recreation activities, public transport, libraries, etc. In order to retain such functions in the local area wholly or in part, one response has been a search for new forms of collaboration through volunteering, shared service delivery, asset transfer and the use of new modes of service delivery such as community organisations, mutuals, co-operatives and social enterprises, as well as a variety of private sector service delivery and property and housing development. By the end of the present Parliament, many critics believe local government will find it difficult to sustain its remaining statutory activities in adult and children's services as well as leaving many local communities and disadvantaged groups vulnerable to the continuing consequences of policies such as welfare reform and benefits cuts (Conrad, 2019).

The loss of experienced professional staff, traditional departments and the fragmentation of service delivery by a variety of agencies, trusts and partnerships in policy areas like education, is making it far more difficult to provide 'seamless' joined-up services such as special education services, capable of tackling cross cutting policy and agency issues. Such problems are being increasingly experienced in fields, such as homelessness, ageing, pensioner isolation, workless-ness, educational attainment, public health, child poverty and the existence of various forms of discrimination. Moreover, against the background of further cuts local authorities are more challenged in providing community and place leadership and a single voice for their areas.

In recent years, the public policy domain has become increasingly fragmented with an array of bodies, some under local democratic control, others directly accountable to central government or with appointed representation. A recent study supported by ILG of governance structures in the North East has highlighted the difficulties this presents (Robinson, Shaw, & Regan, 2017).

In all these respects the ILG model has shown how collaboration between North East academics, practitioners, partners and stakeholders can provide joined-up analyses and solutions reflecting the Partnership's shared vision of 'supporting innovation, improvement, efficiency and quality in public services' (Mawson, 2019).

EMERGING TRENDS IN PLACE BASED KNOWLEDGE EXCHANGE

There is no single formula for the development of knowledge exchange and research collaboration between higher education institutions and local partners (Nutley, Walter, & Davies, 2007). In many parts of the country, the single Civic University model has been developed fitting the geography of place and longstanding economic, social, community and cultural relations (Goddard, Hazelkorn, Kempton, & Vallance, 2016). This tradition is reflected in the so-called 'Red Brick' Universities set up in the second half of the nineteenth century which pioneered new academic and professional disciplines such as Town Planning, Public Health, Social Work and Civil Engineering. The longstanding presence of Universities in their localities is increasingly seen as one key focus in economic development, social, environmental and sustainable development. Newcastle University, for example, has been pioneering proactive and strategic relations with its city region and local community as reflected in the Civic Futures and Civic University programme (Goddard & Tewdwr-Jones, 2016). The North East's post-1992 universities: Northumbria, Sunderland and Teesside have long been individually actively engaged in local research collaboration as exemplified in the case of the Higher Education Funding Council programme on urban regeneration, managed by Northumbria University (MacNamara, 2012). Recently, Tees Valley and North of Tyne Combined Authorities with Mayoral leadership have begun to incorporate University research into the development and delivery of their strategies.

THE RATIONALE FOR THE DEVELOPMENT OF THE ILG

Turning to the ILG, it emerged from a lengthy dialogue in the second half of the last decade concerning the contribution of North East Universities to the increasing challenges faced by public policy and management bodies in the region. At the time, bodies such as the Association of North East Councils,

Universities for the North and other bodies including the Regional Development Agency (One North East) recognised that there were common interests in the pursuit of research and intelligence in the sphere of local and regional governance. It was also acknowledged that the two worlds of academia and practice sometimes draw on different forms of knowledge (tacit – based on practice experience; codified – drawing on formal research processes and publications) and that this presented a potential opportunity to generate new insights based on a two-way flow of knowledge and experience. The so-called 'Co-production of Knowledge Processes' (Pettigrew, 2001) in which there may be engagement with users at all stages of the research process from initial scoping through to delivery and dissemination, is a central feature of how the ILG has worked.

In taking forward these ideas of co-production, the partners recognised that there can be a range of organisational barriers to knowledge exchange which may need to be addressed (Mawson, 2011). Universities, for example, are not always effective at signposting their expertise particularly beyond the non-science and technology areas. In the realm of the public sector, there is evidence that practitioners do not always understand how to engage in and utilise University research (Lowther, 2015). This has been tackled in ILG processes by identifying 'link persons' in each University, strengthening higher level corporate commitment in local authorities to an agreed research agenda, bringing together academics and practitioners in research dialogue through various formal and informal events and partnership arrangements and a 'light touch' support role to practitioners, if necessary, as the research process proceeded.

A further issue which was addressed in designing the ILG model concerned how to put in place a critical mass of academic expertise which needed to be available to service the wide-ranging requirements of public sector organisations. It was recognised that it would be difficult for anyone University within the ILG Partnership to provide the necessary full range of expertise in local governance. Further, there was often a lack of awareness of world class relevant research capacity present locally, hence the need to establish a 'virtual' institute, drawing together and promoting research capacity present in all the Universities of the North East. While the ILG's strategy of encouraging and facilitating local sourcing was designed to improve access to high quality and cost-effective research and intelligence, it was also recognised that the activity could serve to promote a key sector in the North East's regional economy – higher education.

THE ROLE AND FUNCTIONS OF THE ILG MODEL – COLLABORATION AND COMPETITION

It was agreed that the ILG should function as an 'intermediary' or 'bridging agency', whose role would be to facilitate and secure the delivery of the research requirements of its public sector partners through the facilitation of collaboration between practitioners and the relevant academics concerned (Mawson, 2015). The approach was based on the recognition that there are potentially several stages through which knowledge could be developed in a co-production process, leading to research specification and followed by application and dissemination. While not all stages might be followed, and there could be iterative steps, this provided the basis for the ILG process. Once a research brief had been agreed with a public sector partner, the ILG would invite North East academics to bid for the work through an internally organised partnership competition, overseen by the Institute. The public sector partner concerned then selected the successful University supplier(s).

A small ILG team of three academic/professional staff, with senior experience in University research and public sector management, were to be hosted by Durham University in its Business School, but accountable for its activities to the partnership. The activities were to be funded by annual subscription added to by any grant income secured. It would be overseen by a Management Board, chaired on a rotating basis by Local Authority Chief Executives, with senior representatives from the partners and University, including the Dean of the Business School.

A key strength of the ILG partnership has proved to be the robustness of its Constitution which has enabled senior partners on the Management Board to provide a leadership role in adapting to the various vicissitudes of the past decade and cushion the core delivery activities from potentially destabilising external events. Examples include the loss of strategic regional public sector partners, a reduction in funding and shifts in higher education research and funding criteria, as well as the turnover of key influential individuals in the ILG network. By formalising agreed research, knowledge exchange and co-production processes leading to the successful delivery of research projects, the form of partnership management has served to build up mutual understanding of organisational and cultural similarities and differences. It has also made possible informal engagement and dialogue between researchers and practitioners without the need for prior approval from their senior management and organisations, thereby facilitating the development of ideas surrounding new projects.

The following section summarises some of the outputs of the ILG Partnership over the past decade.

ILG ACTIVITIES IN THE NORTH EAST 2009–2019

Since the establishment of the ILG in 2009 it has:

- Secured the delivery of some 100 research projects by North East University academics for its public sector partners worth over £2 million, including some 26 projects delivered directly by the ILG Team.

- Levered over £1 million of extra research funding for the Partnership from Research Councils, Charitable Trusts, voluntary organisations and central and local government.

- Initiated and funded the delivery of major region-wide 'impact' studies for North East Councils and other public sector partners on, for example, Scottish Devolution, Welfare Reform, Public Expenditure cuts, Mental Health Services for Young People, Child Poverty, Public Sector Procurement policies re SMEs, Procurement as a means to secure 'quality employment' in the North East.

- Contributed to North East Sub-Regional and Devolution agendas by: (1) providing technical support to public opinion surveys on Devolution in County Durham and Teesside; (2) undertaking for Tees Valley Combined Authority, a review of public accountability mechanisms in comparable bodies; (3) developing a strategy to encourage economic collaboration and networks between Northern England and the Scottish Border; (4) evaluated a national pilot project for the North East Ambulance and Fire Services to facilitate collaboration on emergency services; and (5) compared the characteristics of emerging models of metropolitan local government in the UK and France.

- With regard to local economic development, contributions have included: the economic opportunities of Devolution for the North; delivering research projects on evaluating the long-term impact of capital projects in Teesside; examining the economic, social and community consequences of large-scale plant closure in Northumberland; assessing Redcar and Cleveland's enterprise activities for the long-term unemployed; and Gateshead Council's apprenticeship scheme; identifying potential growth clusters; and the impact of wind farms on tourism for Northumberland County Council.

- Over 150 North East academics from the region's five Universities have been involved in delivering projects representing a wide range of academic disciplines, with some 21 projects involving two or more North East Universities as well as working with York, York St John, Huddersfield and Cumbria Universities and University College London. Where local university experience has not been present (only very occasionally), the ILG has also drawn on 'think tanks' and specialist consultancies, for example, Shared Intelligence, Segal Quince Wickstead and IPPR North. This has given academics the opportunity to work alongside consultants and extend their contacts and networks.

- Since its initiation in 2009, the ILG has run various 'out of office' fora, or 'spaces of communication' bringing together academics and practitioners to explore common policy, practice and research issues: ILG-Fuse Public Health Partnership; the North East Regional Information Network; the Crime and Community Safety Partnership; and the North East Child Poverty Commission – all of which have generated research contributing to policy and practice over extended periods.

- In disseminating the outcome of its activities over 210 workshops, seminars and conferences involving some 5,500 academics and practitioners have been held across the North East, yielding consistently high delegate evaluation scores. In these events senior academics and practitioners from across the UK with senior figures from

North East business organisations, the public, voluntary and charity sectors, and senior local government politicians. Specific annual themes have been pursued covering, for example, 'public services at a time of austerity' and 'local economic development'. A shorter series of two or three events have been held on topics such as arts and culture in economic, social and environmental development, recycling and waste management and the circular economy.

- The findings of the above studies have been utilised and reported to the House of Common and House of Lords Select Committees, the Scottish and European Parliaments, and various government departments and agencies such as the National Audit Office.

THE NORTHUMBRIA CONTRIBUTION

A more specific illustration of the nature of University-practitioner collaboration can be made by drawing on the participation of Northumbria University and its academic community in the work of the ILG (Mawson, 2019). Over the past decade this has involved delivering 25 research projects, including eight undertaken jointly with two or more other North East Universities. Work has been carried out for the Department of Work and Pensions; six local authorities (Redcar and Cleveland, Middlesbrough, South Tyneside, North Tyneside, Gateshead and Northumberland) together with region-wide work for the Association of North East Councils. Northumbria academics working singly or with other North East Universities have delivered: maximising the benefits of Scottish Devolution for the region; the development of a Borderlands Strategy; the consequences of Brexit for the rural north; the relevance of the National Planning Framework in addressing housing need in the North East, and the impact of welfare reform across the North East.

More specific projects for individual partners have also addressed a wide range of topics, for example: employee engagement and organisational resilience; measuring and improving the culture of the workplace; evaluation of a local authority apprenticeship scheme; assessment of community initiatives and social enterprise; innovative approaches to the provision of adult social care; routes to employability for offenders and alternatives to prison for women offenders.

Academic staff in Northumbria have also regularly attended, participated in and hosted ILG seminars (Mawson, 2019).

ASSESSMENT OF THE ILG: PROS AND CONS

The establishment of the ILG was undoubtedly ambitious in geographical scope and range of activities and the require-ment for a multidisciplinary approach. One of the leading researchers in this field, Professor Sandra Nutley, in her book *Using Evidence: How Research can inform Public Services* (2007) comments:

> *interactive approaches currently seem to show*
> *most promise in achieving use of research ... this*
> *often involves collaboration or partnership with*
> *local Universities and/or intermediary research*
> *organisations .... Evaluations of research-practice*
> *partnerships conclude that collaborative approaches*
> *have proved successful. However, most such*
> *activities are small scale in focus with limited*
> *geographical scope .... scaling up such an activity so*
> *that it encompasses the majority of service delivery*

> *organisations across a range of sectors is likely to*
> *prove challenging if not impractical. (pp. 127–128)*

The comment on 'scaling up' is perhaps suggestive of what has been achieved by the ILG given the geographical extent of its activities, the involvement of a multiplicity of public sector organisations, and the engagement of private, voluntary and community sectors in its work.

Positive feedback on the quality and impact of ILG's work has come from independent surveys of academic and practice communities, while a national survey for the ESRC, Local Government Association and SOLACE has commented:

> *Some characteristics emerge in terms of 'what*
> *works' ... in the case of the role of research and*
> *knowledge exchange intermediaries both the ILG*
> *and Sheffield RESS are shining lights that point the*
> *way. (Allen, 2014)*

While there are positive outcomes from the work of the ILG, it must be remembered that it has been a pioneering initiative which has never attempted before in this form. A key issue as highlighted by Professor Nutley remains the difficulty of managing such an ambitious project in terms of the scope of activities, geographical spread and co-ordination in a multiagency decision-making context with institutions with distinctively different organisational cultures.

In the original design agreed by the partners in 2008, senior academics pointed out that a minimum number of six staff were required to achieve high quality academic outputs from the team.

In the event a budget of a third less than originally planned, due to financial pressures faced by partners resulted in the cutting of two posts and the freezing of partner subscriptions from 2013 onwards. A related problem has been the changing attitudes of key partners among the University sector. When thinking around the establishment of the ILG model, this occurred at the end of the Labour Government when regional collaboration including higher education was a priority and the REF and the concept of impact case studies had yet to emerge. However, over the following decade, performance measures in terms of research outputs have prioritised a competitive environment in which collaborative approaches have become relatively less attractive. While public sector membership of the partnership barely changed and more and more academics and practitioners participated in its work, successively Universities withdrew until in 2019 Durham University decided to no longer host the initiative because the ILG agenda did not fit into its long-term research priorities. The University did formally acknowledge its valuable work in promoting the external engagement and profile of Durham and other North East Universities. The ILG was, however, able to maintain its activities because it has built upon an active 'research-practice community of interest', which has involved North East University academics continuing to bid for ILG projects and participate in its knowledge exchange activities and events across the region (Amin & Roberts, 2008).

In summarising, it would be a mistake to discuss the experience of this initiative purely on sustainability grounds because of its ambition at a time of severe financial constraint and institutional retrenchment. It is contended that it does provide many important and practical insights into academic-practice collaboration. The ILG represents a model capable of adopting a wider strategic approach to research collaboration, transcending local administrative boundaries and cross cutting issues. This is exemplified in the operational design of the ESRC-Welsh Assembly Public Policy Centre hosted at Cardiff Business School, which consciously drew on the ILG model.

REFLECTIONS ON THE WAY FORWARD
AND POST-BREXIT

At a time of financial pressures on research budgets in both public sector and higher education institutions the loss of research staff and organisational capacity; and the emergence of new local governance structures transcending individual local authority boundaries – the challenges of research collaboration is ever more to the fore. A Local Government Chronicle survey in February 2015 identified some 40 existing and emerging strategic cross-boundary partnerships stimulated by the evolving devolution agenda in England (Paine, 2015). In addressing this agenda, it is likely that this will entail increased inter-authority and University research collaboration. Experience has shown that there are a range of approaches that can be deployed in this context ranging, for example, from a single University to local authority initiative to larger scale private, voluntary or community research partnerships; to sub-regional working with County or City Region arrangements; cross-border research collaboration and full blown regional partnership working.

The latter approach is undoubtedly more difficult to put in place and manage since it involves more partners, formal and informal relationships and has resource implications. Nevertheless, we would argue that variants of the ILG approach and processes could be adapted to varying circumstances on a cost-effective basis.

Such approaches can develop shared economies of scale and scope in research capacity and the development of ongoing policy and practice research priorities contributing to the strategies of Combined Authorities, Local Enterprise Partnerships and the National Industrial Strategy. The approach makes possible local institutions being engaged throughout the research process, developing joint ownership of the proposals and ensuring 'local fit'. Rather than utilising consultant 'off the shelf' products, local research collaboration embeds local knowledge, expertise and organisational capacity. As Marlow (2015) comments in a Local Government Information Unit review of the current evolving landscape:

> there is a strong case for consortia of local authorities to engage collectively and coherently with major Universities whose impact and influence is likely to be sub-regional and regional in character …. Given the pivotal and likely increasing role of HEIs and LEP-based local growth programmes, there is an immediate rationale for this level of deliberative exchange. (p. 7)

ACKNOWLEDGEMENTS

Professor John Mawson served as the Director of the Institute for Local Governance between 2009 and 2019 and wishes to acknowledge, on behalf of the Partnership, the support provided by the ESRC Collaborative Ventures Scheme, the North East Improvement and Efficiency Partnership, and Durham University and its Business School in hosting the Institute. He would also like to acknowledge all those practitioners in the public, private, voluntary and community sectors, his ILG colleagues and the academics from the five North East Universities who enthusiastically engaged in the work of the ILG.

12

THE FUTURE OF PUBLIC ADMINISTRATION TEACHING AND RESEARCH IN THE NORTH EAST

Ian C. Elliott and Lorraine Johnston

INTRODUCTION

The purpose of this chapter is to explore the role of universities in the post-Brexit North East. Specifically, it is noted that Brexit has uncovered (or heightened) significant grievances towards metropolitan elites (whether they be in Westminster or Brussels). There is, in many respects, a sense of the left behind – with an ever-powerful Westminster to the south and an emerging force in Holyrood to the north. There have, in recent years, been moves towards addressing some of these apparent grievances with measures such as English Votes for English Laws (EVEL), development of the Northern Powerhouse, introduction of combined authorities and locally elected mayors within major cities and Local Industrial Strategies.

At the same time Brexit is likely to require further investment in governance systems and mechanisms across the UK.

This chapter begins by exploring aspects of the Brexit vote and highlights some of the underpinning grievances that may have influenced the significant leave vote from North East constituencies. This section ends by recognising the peculiar position of universities within the region. The second section then explores the response to Brexit both in relation to regional governance and in respect of universities. It is noted that universities within the North East may have a significant role to play in a post-Brexit devolved public sector landscape. In this context it is found that Northumbria University has a unique position with a long-established track record of teaching and research in public administration.

Overall it is found that ongoing constitutional changes pose significant opportunities and threats to universities within the North East. This region of England has a particularly high number of universities which contribute highly to the regional economy and to employment. Yet at the same time these same universities are especially dependent on links with other European countries, and to the EU, in relation to research funding, staffing and students. These existing and long-standing links may help to limit any negative impact of Brexit. They may also provide an important role as anchor institutions for further regional development and multilevel governance systems.

In this regard, Northumbria University has an enviable position as the regional centre of excellence in the teaching and research of public administration. Developments such as the new Senior Leaders Master's Degree Apprenticeship in Strategic Leadership for Public Services demonstrate the capacity within the university to foster links across and within sectors, to help bridge the skills shortage across public services, and to nurture boundary-spanning leadership capabilities.

THE CONUNDRUM OF BREXIT

The Result

Research published after the referendum result has naturally focussed on the causes of Brexit with arguments centring on the many potential causes of the leave vote. These have highlighted age, social attitudes and education as significant factors that represent the 'left behind' who were particularly pro-Brexit (Dorling, Stuart, & Stubbs, 2016; Goodwin & Heath, 2016). Others have highlighted how the leave vote was the culmination of long-standing public and intraparty divisions particularly over the issue of Europe (Menon & Salter, 2016). Interestingly, many of these divisions and antecedents of the Brexit vote have not been resolved in the three years following the result and in fact have led to more uncertainty and political turmoil as a number of UK Prime Ministers, and many more Brexit Secretaries, have worked towards negotiating the eventual withdrawal of the UK from the EU.

It is widely recognised within the research that the nature of the Brexit vote was highly complex. In particular, it must be stressed that there is no single UK picture that can account for the Brexit vote as Northern Ireland and Scotland both voted, along with London and Gibraltar, to remain (Harris & Charlton, 2016). Even with England, the largest constituent of the UK, there is a mixed picture when we consider the regions.

As shown by Harris and Charlton (2016) the West Midlands, East Midlands and North East were the three most pro-leave regions but there are also significant variations within these regions. Elsewhere it has been shown that areas which voted predominantly for leaving the EU are also those which have, over the decades, benefitted most from EU funding (Los et al., 2017). Therefore, it may be assumed that they will also be those who will lose most though others have made the case that the areas which voted remain will be hardest hit economically from Brexit (Dhingra, Machin, & Overman, 2017).

In the North East, as with other regions, there were many different and complex factors which influenced the vote to leave. Rushton (2017) accepts that cosmopolitanism, educational level and local community diversity all influenced voter behaviour. Yet they also highlight that some areas within the North East, such as Teeside, voted very differently to what might be expected given levels of community diversity in that area.

Whatever the reasons for Brexit they are likely, as suggested by Menon and Salter (2016), to have historical and deep-seeded routes. Here we can identify three important factors that have been found to be contributing factors to the leave vote at a regional level – the North–South economic divide; the impact of austerity on the North and a form of democratic deficit.

North–South Divide

The privatisation of national industries of ship building, coal and steel which occurred from the 1980s onwards had a particularly devastating effect on the North of England, Wales and Scotland. Where the focus on boosting the financial services industry provided a significant boost to London there was no such equivalent across other regions of the UK. In other words, Thatcherism exacerbated regional inequalities throughout the UK (Hudson & Williams, 1995; Jessop, Bonnett, Bromley, & Ling, 1988; Lewis & Townsend, 1989). These regional inequalities have been shown to map closely to the referendum results – with economically disadvantaged areas returning the largest 'leave' vote (Harris & Charlton, 2016).

Some progress was made under the Labour Governments of 1997–2008 to narrow this divide and by 2005, unemployment in northern regions had gone down to the national average of 5% (Johnson, 2015b). Yet there is evidence to suggest that regions such as the North East were particularly badly hit by the recession and have made particularly slow recovery since (Johnson, 2015a). Others note that Brexit is likely to exacerbate regional inequalities even further (Billing, McCann, & Ortega-Argiles, 2019) due to the lack of existing sub-national governance mechanisms or regional economic development activity which might otherwise have limited these effects. It is also widely accepted that regions including the North East that voted to leave at also those that benefit most from EU membership (Los, McCAnn, Springford, & Thissen, 2017).

Impact of Austerity

It is estimated that jobs in the public sector or dependent on public funding accounted for 73.1% of all new jobs created in the North East between 1998 and 2007 (Erturk, Froud, Johal, Leaver, & Willliams, 2012). This is in comparison to only 32.8% of new jobs created in London (Erturk et al., 2012). The dependence on public finance for new job creation in the North East during this time is seen to be the product of de-industrialisation which had happened in the previous decades while London, in particular, benefited from a large expansion in the banking and finance sector. GDP growth during this time was also greater in London than in the North East (Martin, Pike, Tyler, & Gardiner, 2016) and wage inequality between the regions grew (Elliott, 2017).

Democratic Deficit

Finally, there is a sense of disenfranchisement as combination of the above plus seeing extra powers in Scotland and Wales as well as devolution in Northern Ireland (though not working) and London. There is significant literature documenting the rise and fall of regional governance in the North East (Robinson et al., 2000; Robinson & Shaw, 1994; Shaw & Robinson, 2011; Shaw & Robinson, 2012). The dismantling of regional governance systems and mechanisms in the North East has contributed to a sense of democratic deficit (Shaw & Robinson, 2018). It is noted that,

> *It is hard enough for a North East of 2.6 million*
> *people and only 29 MPs to make an impact in a*
> *highly centralised structure centred on London*
> *some 250 miles away. It is even harder for three*
> *Combined Authorities each to get a hearing, while*
> *the local authorities, battered by austerity, have*
> *almost no influence. (p. 848)*

This is mirrored by Jeffery, Wyn Jones, Henderson, Scully, and Lodge (2014), who showed how Scotland were seen to have preserved advantages as a result of the devolution settlement as well as a degree of resentment towards the EU.

The North East is again significant in this context as it was the only region to hold a referendum on the establishment of a directly elected regional assembly (which was very significantly rejected by 77.9% the electorate). Yet there continue to be calls for greater regional devolution and policy has already shifted with the development of Devolution Deals, the Northern Powerhouse agenda and legislation on EVEL (Giovanni, 2016).

The Role of Universities

Brexit poses particular implications for universities. In this section we will explore the current context of universities in the North East before going on, in the next section, to consider how best universities might respond to these particular challenges.

Across the UK it is widely recognised that universities benefit greatly from UK membership of the European Union. Universities across the UK receive £1 billion a year through programmes such as Horizon 2020 and as much as 19.7% of all research and development funding comes from outside the country, particularly from the EU (Marginson, 2017).

Within the North East region there are five universities (Durham, Newcastle, Northumbria, Teeside and Sunderland) as well as over 20 colleges. The five universities in the region employ over 14,000 staff and generate another 15,000 jobs through their activities (Universities UK, 2014). The impact of Brexit is significant as it is estimated that a significant proportion of staff, and particularly research-active staff, at these universities are non-UK EU nationals. Estimates suggest that up to 18% of staff employed by some universities in the North East are non-UK EU nationals (North East Brexit Group, 2018). The economic value of universities in the North East is estimated to be a gross value added (GVA) of nearly £1.6 billion, equivalent to 3.8% of the total 2011 North East GVA (Universities UK, 2014). This is higher than in any other region of England meaning that any threat to the UK university sector represents a disproportionately greater threat to the North East economy.

It has been noted for some time that universities have an important regional role (Charles, 2003) and that new universities in particular are already making contributions to local and regional development (Glasson, 2003). In this regard, there has been growing interest in the idea of universities as anchor institutions (Goddard, Coombes, Kempton, & Vallance, 2014) and their potential role in developing place-based leadership and regional development activities (Colledge, 2015). This role would seem to be particularly important in the North East where it has been shown that universities disproportionally highly compared to other regions. How universities may respond to these challenges is the focus of the next section.

WHAT NEXT FOR UNIVERSITIES IN THE NORTH EAST?

The Resurgence of Regionalism

The prominence of constitutional issues within UK politics, as symbolised by both the Scottish Independence Referendum in 2014 and the EU Referendum in 2016, has intensified calls for greater devolution within England (and indeed greater devolved powers for Scotland, Wales and Northern Ireland). In the case of England, the Scottish Independence Referendum was quickly followed by calls from the then Prime Minister David Cameron for EVEL in 2014 (Jeffery et al., 2014). This was included in the UK Conservative Party manifesto for the General Election in 2015 and new procedures to allow for MP's representing English constituencies to have a veto on laws only affecting England were approved by the UK Parliament in October 2015.

The sense that 'metropolitan elites' of London were the main beneficiaries of EU membership was perpetrated widely as part of the Leave campaign in 2016 (Billing et al., 2019). Such claims were later proven to be false (Los et al., 2017) but served to highlight the sense of disillusionment among some at the sense of disenfranchisement and reflect a long-standing dissatisfaction at how England is governed within the UK (Jeffery et al., 2014).

In this context significant powers were devolved to the Manchester City Region in 2014–2015. The Greater Manchester Combined Authority (GMCA), encompassing 10 local authorities, had been in place since 2011 but further powers have been devolved since then, arguably in response to the Scottish referendum (Fenwick, 2015; Kenealy, 2016). Undoubtedly GMCA remains a model that dominates discussion around Combined Authorities although not always well received by others (Shutt & Liddle, 2019b). Following the model set out by Manchester Fenwick and Elcock (2018) note that further devolution of powers is likely even if a fully federalised UK is impossible to envisage.

Although much has changed since both referendums of 2014 and 2016 in relation to the development of combined authorities, elected mayors and local industrial strategies it has been argued that their development has been 'nascent and patchy' (Dickinson & Cox, 2016, p. 3). Others have described the development of combined authorities as 'prolonged and patchy' (Liddle & Shutt, 2019, p. 91). The Institute for Public Policy Research (IPPR) have argued that Combined Authorities located in the North of England should cooperate within a new Northern Brexit Negotiating Committee (Dickinson & Cox, 2016). Others have highlighted how greater devolution of powers to the regions is essential within a post-Brexit UK but that Brexit itself is 'leading to both further governance centralization and also the stalling of many policy arenas' (Billing et al., 2019, p. 757). Within this it is important to consider the role that universities may play.

HE REFORMS AND THE CHALLENGE OF BREXIT

In a context of Brexit, UK government has sought to mitigate university risk through the development of Higher Education policies that seek to secure the future of the university sector.

The Higher Education White Paper – *Success as a Knowledge Economy: Teaching Excellence, Social Mobility and Student Choice* (DBIS, 2016) exemplifies a need for universities to thrive in Brexit. In considering the consequences of Brexit on the UK higher education sector, Mayhew (2017, §156) predicts a number of facets comprising of 'massive uncertainty' and 'several areas of threat' that drive reflection. Four overarching pressures have been identified in relation to universities post-Brexit: the number of EU students in the UK; access to research funding; ability to attract staff from EU countries; and the ability of UK students to study abroad (Corbett, 2016; MacKay, 2016; Mayhew, 2017).

More recently the Review of Post-18 Education and Funding, known as the Augar Review after the panel chair, has recommended changes especially in relation to the funding of higher education. The recommendations include reducing tuition fees, extending the repayment period and reducing the income threshold for tuition loan repayments and reintroducing maintenance grants for disadvantaged students. The impact on universities would be felt most in areas such as the North East (where graduate salaries are typically lower than in London and the South East) as well as in courses relating to the public sector, such as nursing. Yet the recommendations have yet to be adopted by the UK Government and within the Cabinet there would seem to be a range of views. For example, Jo Johnson MP, the current Minister of State at the Department for Business, Energy and Industrial Strategy and Department for Education, recently tweeted:

> *Augar (as predicated) will destabilise university finances, imperil many courses & reverse progress in widening access. Reducing fees to £7.5k will leave funding hole HMT won't fill + benefit only highest earning grads at expense of general taxpayer. Bad policy, bad politics. (Johnson, 2019)*

At the same time Universities UK have argued for a wide range of measures that the UK Government must put in place prior to Brexit. These include acting to support EU students and staff, ensure access to research funding is sustained, and

> *[...] creating a UK Shared Prosperity Fund (UKSPF) that is informed by the expertise and experience of universities, sufficiently accounting for devolved / regional need. (Universities UK, 2018)*

With the later of these measures we can see how universities may play a greater role within regional governance structures post-Brexit.

Universities UK have also suggested a greater role for degree apprenticeships arguing that

> *the system should develop to meet current and future demand for higher level skills in areas such as digital technology, management, public services, and to boost regional economies. [emphasis added] (Universities UK, 2019, p. 3)*

This includes a recommendation that degree apprenticeships are embedded within local industrial strategies. The skills shortages currently experienced across the public sector, including in health, social care and policing, are likely to be exacerbated by Brexit and so the role of degree apprenticeships may become even more important.

University Responses to Brexit

The North East Universities response to Brexit and fluctuations in the market have sought to transform branch campuses towards the expansion of university activities through extending outreach and third mission activities. As such universities have established campuses within EU countries (Adams, 2016). Universities have begun to integrate strategic economic planning in mission statements and envisage a coherent response to regional economic development growth need and impact. Boxall (2016) argues that universities will increase competition in an attempt to diminish any negative economic growth impact post-Brexit. Further Boxall (2016) asserts that universities can strengthen existing regional European partnerships through providing a more extensive role for participant engagement in ensuring much greater benefits for regional devolution are realised. As strategic leaders, universities have begun to facilitate economic growth through evolving research and knowledge capabilities that accelerate innovation and public sector entrepreneurship (Cunningham & Link, 2015). Likewise, advancing local and regional industrial strategies for technology transfer (Cunningham, Lehmann, Menter, & Seitz, 2019) and digital technologies evolve diverse partnerships that safeguard more rapid collaborations with governments, public services, businesses and the third sector. These collaborations seek to build evidence-based research opportunities that advance collective problem-solving in overcoming regional economic challenges.

North East universities adopting strategic leadership roles will aim to strengthen relations with European partners in creating wider research networks that enable transnational knowledge flows. Moving beyond the boundaries of local and regional economic development strategies is an attempt to close cultural and diversity gaps between universities, business and governments. The North East Universities response to overcoming regional economic development barriers will be to facilitate innovative and local enterprise partnerships. These partnerships are known to evolve mutual interactions with external local and global partner organisations, public agencies and industry to advance the 'knowledge economy'. Examples of university–industry linkages and entrepreneurial activities to advance research and knowledge interactions between university researchers and industry illustrate benefits can be gained (Boardman, 2009; D'Este & Patel, 2007). Initiatives to enhance productivity (Lee & Bozeman, 2005) advance university engaging with industry collaborations as science parks to advance innovation and science based technologies (Marques, Caraca, & Diz, 2006; Meyer-Krahmer & Schmoch, 1998), university interactions with business to advance applied research (Balconi & Laboranti, 2006), as well enterprise incubator support services and Living Labs which act as intermediaries for institutions seeking to commercialise Intellectual Property through engagement in 'open innovation' business models (Chesbrough, 2006). Examples include Porter's clusters that enable university business knowledge transfer including Science Parks, Business Incubators, Technology Transfer Offices, Catapult Centres (Wilson, 2012) all of which strive to find solutions to regional problems.

The Case of Northumbria University

There are a number of initiatives within Northumbria University which demonstrate how universities may operate within these new multilevel governance systems as anchor institutions for regional development.

Northumbria University's Business Clinic demonstrates university business engagement through offering students the opportunity to work on a live industry problem. These diverse partnerships offer mutual respect where students can work on a consultancy project that provides a solution to a problem. This mode advances student capabilities in learning applied skills as well as enhancing student prospects for employability and graduate retention after graduation of key skills in the North East city region.

In 2017, to boost low skills aspiration and drive ambition and increase productivity the UK government introduced the apprenticeship levy for employers. Developing a higher level skills base was a key requirement of the Wilson Review

The prospect for university regional engagement needs to build on local regional strengths, universities increasingly operate with a variety of sectors and business to facilitate student entrepreneurship including providing facilities for business through start-up grants. Since 2012, Northumbria University has seen an increase in the development of enterprise and entrepreneurship programmes. An increase in new forms of university business interactions as regional businesses, local authorities, combined authorities, charities and mayor models to advance universities role in civic society engagement.

To counter this, North East universities have begun to embed locally in city regions and influence communities in their role of anchor institutions (Wilson, 2012). Anchor institutions provide cultural benefits and build on historical past and key strengths of the city region to encourage regional growth and academic entrepreneurship.

Examples of universities in the North East taking on regional development competitive roles has seen an increase in local collaborations with business markets with uncertainty of BREXIT have begun to take on regional identities through greater collaboration.

CONCLUSION

In conclusion, Brexit continues to threaten to challenge the long-term position, mission and sustainability of the university sector in the North East. Much anxiety over competition and the long-term roles for the uniqueness of North East Universities remain, yet Northumbria University is leading the way in building on the success of *Public Management and Public Policy* (3PM) Research Interest Group which hosts important public events, bringing academic research closer to practice. Examples of 3PM research seminars include Little Heresies Talks as well as hosting the JUC Annual Conference 2018 and 2019. This has begun to extend the university role as lead provider of innovative education through engagement in government apprenticeship programmes as the MSc Strategic Leadership for Public Leadership which continues to strengthen partnership working with employers and agencies across the region. These innovative modules are CMI certified, professionally relevant and academically robust SLMDA programme. This places Northumbria in unique place as centre for excellence in 3PM. The expansion of university mission and strategic role in regional economic growth offers engagement with local communities. Greater emphasis has placed on Northumbria University high in the rankings and maintained their capabilities to extend their teaching and research reach beyond regional economic growth.

13

DEVELOPING A NEW
FOCUS ON FUTURE RESEARCH
FOR THE REGION

John Shutt and Joyce Liddle

This policy pivot is being published in the autumn of 2019. The editors have no idea what the outcome of the Boris Johnson UK Conservative administration will be at the time of writing, but we are anticipating a 'No Deal' Brexit on the 31 October 2019.

A 'No Deal' Brexit will have grave implications for the North East economy which is already weak and Cabras has highlighted the many issues in Chapter 4 of this book. It may now be that the Boris Johnson Conservative government does manage to get its new Deal done with the European Commission and that this is passed by the UK parliament. At the time of writing we do not yet know how this Brexit moment will proceed and a British General Election and/or a second referendum could well be the only way to proceed to bring closure to the Brexit period since 2016. Either way uncertainty is increasing and the UK's inequalities are increasing and attention is on Brexit not on the resolution of public policy issues and the improvement of public services. Moreover, a negotiated Deal may in fact accelerate the break-up of the United Kingdom with Scotland accelerating its independence and others arguing for a United Ireland and a federal United Kingdom as long term solutions.. Either way, *Deal or No Deal* the future of regions and Places is set to become more centre stage and Brexit is not going to go away in the decade ahead.

The Brexit Party argues that a £200bn programme of regional investment is needed for the North of England and many people are focussed on trying to elaborate how the UK Shared Prosperity Fund can deliver for towns and cities that are losing out; in particular, the key cities outside of the Core Cities that so desperately need fresh investment and new policies and programmes to shift deep-seated social, economic and environmental problems. The Conservative Party has suddenly announced a shift from austerity to increased public expenditure growth and has announced new commitments to health, education, police and post-BREXIT funding for Key cities - The Stronger Towns Fund.

On their own these new funds will not tackle these deep-seated and fundamental problems, and the Brexit dividend will fail to materialise. In order to tackle the problems of Regional and Urban leadership, governance, devolution and regional economic development this needs a clearer plan for the region as a whole and for the rest of England. Additionally, a clearer view is required of the future and potential of the Northern Powerhouse and how it sits with the new City-region Combined Authorities, such as Tees Valley and the North of Tyne. Headlam, Shutt and Liddle debate how this might be achieved in Chapters 1 and 2 of this book.

In the Brexit moment we need more critical reflections on changing work and labour markets in the North East region and identification of key processes that drive localities. There is still a tendency to regard the private sector as a key source of jobs but the danger of ignoring the role of the public and voluntary sectors has been evident for some time since the Coalition government of 2010 abandoned the Cameron mantra of Localism. Chapter 3 brings out the centrality of the NHS to this region and its key role in future employment and service delivery. The NHS Plan must have its regional investment plans integrated into debates surrounding employment, economic development policy and investment plans, and further elaborated in the pursuit of changing the fortunes of communities. We need a regional NHS Plan to be integrated with local government and Third Sector priorities, especially now that health investment has been earmarked for a key role in investment plans.

Our analysis of multilevel and 'contested governance' in the North East highlights complex realities which are repeated in the North West and Yorkshire. There are clear and identifiable key 'wicked' issues and policy tensions between the EU, central government and local government. In the Brexit moment, key European funds will cease to be available after the EU 2014–2020 programme ends, but it would be foolish to think that Europe is becoming irrelevant to the North East. Many key companies are still European controlled and Dutch, Swedish, German and Scandinavian linkages will need to be strengthened and maintained in the period ahead. Regional leaders will need to think these issues through and maintain a clear focus on European collaborations. This will mean the need to focus a move away from siloed thinking towards integration at all levels. Anyone who is concerned with the environment and climate change knows that it is imperative to accelerate European collaboration in the years ahead, whether the focus is on North Sea futures, climate change planning or 2050 Energy targets. Indeed, in Chapter 7, Mordue suggests the need to drive Tourism and Culture in the North East over the next decade will be critical for the region's fortunes and that this is one sector which could benefit from BREXIT. Tourism needs a strong European focus as well as a global one. The region's Scandinavian, Baltic and Dutch links will remain critical – hence the importance of Northumbria University developing the new Amsterdam campus; and the centrality of Newcastle airport and the Port of Tyne.

International policy engagement has begun to favour the UK–USA policy transfer process and many people have high hopes that the American-style super Mayors introduced by the 2010 and 2017 Coalition and Conservative administrations will be capable of driving the change process. In the North East region governance changes are unfinished and contentious, raising issues of what will happen south of the Tyne and of rivalries between the Tyne and the Tees. Some of the latest depreviation data (MHCLG, 2019) shows the Tees local authority districts of Middlesbrough and Hartlepool to be in the most deprived areas nationally. County Councils have frequently felt that they are losing power to the core urban city regions, and the current Brexit situation is exacerbating their problems. The future of the Industrial Strategy and small firms' policies in the new administrations is unclear as is the future of the Local Enterprise Partnerships (LEPs) or transport authorities, and until there is some clarity on such overlapping policies, boundaries and structures in the next policy period, it is true that policy delivery remains uncertain and difficult to coordinate with blurred responsibilities. In Chapter 5 of this book Charles reports on Industrial Strategies and research and investment priorities and in chapter 6 Shaw identifies the latest sub-regional initiative – the BORDERLANDS initiative – a joint approach across the border with the Scottish Parliament and Scottish local authorities, elaborating a new rural Deal for the North. Rusk in Chapter 8 explores small firms and innovation in the North East.

Research on the changing nature of devolution and regional governance, continues to make the case for more adequate funding to achieve success, particularly in the case of the LEPs and local economic development since 2010. This has involved continually identifying the need to rationalise the 70 different national funding streams, managed by 22 government departments and specialist agencies. These attempts at reducing coverage have failed miserably as the scale and levels of complexity continue to escalate. We argue that we need to move beyond devolution and competitive bidding, while continuing to update regional development plans and achieve better synergy, cooperation, rationality and collective learning in the policy-making process.

The policy field of urban and regional development will face new challenges from 2020 and it looks as if 'place-based development' will now feature centre stage in the decade ahead. This change will require a clearer understanding of policy tensions and unresolved policy matters, for example, devolution frameworks, Combined Authority capabilities, to facilitate the next stage of regional development and regional capacity building. Only by continually asking 'what works?' can regional leaders move the policy process forward and improve existing practices. Unfortunately, multidisciplinary and cross boundary working is in short supply and as Wilson, Martin, and Jamieson identify in Chapter 10 these practices have not been easy to introduce into the region. Moreover, in all the changing stakeholder and policy changes we argue that the role of the Universities needs to be better understood and brought into greater play in the period ahead. In Chapter 10, Cunningham identifies the role of public sector entrepreneurship in the universities and argues for a significant role for these regional anchor institutions. In Chapter 11, Mawson highlights the value of developing academic-practitioner networks facilitating research and knowledge exchange.

BOX 13.1. THE LEP 11 EMERGE.

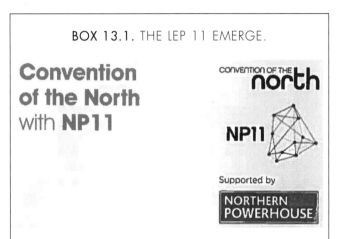

Reflecting on the period of the Coalition and Conservative governments and the shift from Cameron to May to Boris Johnson we believe there are four key areas for future research which must be paramount for the region:

First, is the need for continued local and regional economy analysis at a time when the regional architecture is patchy and many people are worried about the focus on Core cities, to the exclusion of key cities. Moreover, secondary and tertiary local authorities are struggling to cope with the effects of globalisation. A new round of industrial restructuring appears to be about to be launched, through services globalisation, robotic investment and BREXIT uncertainty. Above all else it is important to understand how local strategic employment and skills plans fit into equivalent sub-regional and regional plans and strategies, and how regional plans fit within wider the Northern Powerhouse refreshed Strategy. Despite the development of mayoral groupings and, now LEP Eleven structures there is a lack of clarity in current institutional arrangements.

Second, the BREXIT process and the new programmes arising from it, the stronger Towns Fund, – the UK Shared

Prosperity Fund and the Industrial Strategy Challenge Fund are cases in point, but BREXIT impacts and the decline of multilevel governance will themselves impact differently on local and regional economies, and there is, as yet, a lack of clarity on the policy framework that is evolving. It would help if there was a stronger forum for debate on these issues to guide the region at this current BREXIT moment. It is vital for all regional stakeholders to come together and share knowledge and understandings of the complexity and fragmentation of current governance arrangements and the new funding programmes.

Third, the Combined Authorities, City-Regional governance, and the role of Place Leadership needs further examination. Metro-Mayors and Mayoral Development Corporations are emerging in parts of England, and there is a new rise of mega-regional planning concepts such as The Northern Powerhouse; Midlands Engine; and the Oxford–Cambridge Corridor; all apparently with no clear leadership. Transport and infrastructure planning play a big role here with HS2 and HS3 potentially changing the labour market in key regions, from 2025 onwards. These uncertainties together with delays to the UK and Spending Review will create further uncertainties and ambiguities. There is a need to develop new integrated approaches to policy, which is extremely difficult to achieve given the fragmentation of national infrastructure planning and city region planning. There is a real danger that Yorkshire, the North East and parts of the East and West Midlands will fall even further behind other English regions in the period up to 2030.

A fourth area will be the need to advance international comparative studies in Place Leadership and to enhance understanding of federal and non-federal systems of regional governance and the role of key institutions. It will also be essential to keep a sharp focus on changing EU regional policy for 2020–2027 and its implications for the UK. By contrast, the policies of the BRIICS,[1] which are set to be the UK's new trading partners, will become more pertinent to the future of UK cities, as will the rise of Indian and Chinese cities and those in other emerging economies. It appears that the UK is set to be more international and global, but thus far there is a limited understanding of the importance of future European and global linkages. Universities have been at the forefront in leading of fostering global connections, but the local implications of their international strategies are not well articulated, or fully understood.

Finally, the UK's Industrial Strategy and its future are critical for regional development. The strategy as currently set out is both lame and lacking in ambition, particularly if compared with German, United States or Chinese plans, for example, 'Made in China 2025'. In the coming years, we need more than ever an industrial and new skills strategy which is also spatially aware.

In the decade ahead fresh insights will be needed in economic geography, globalisation and regional governance in the UK to inform a new generation of policy-making. It appears that we are to have a new round of 'Local Industrial Strategies' led by the LEPs and Mayoral Combined Authorities staring in 2019. Local Industrial Strategies on their own are insufficient and sector plans need strong integration into the regional as we have already articulated. It is also important to note that the world is not becoming increasingly global and urban for every community or locality. The intensity and centrality of cities in regional development and the need to acknowledge rurality as part of the overall picture is a significant factor, particularly in the UK and especially in the North East region.

In an era of changing austerity and expanding public expenditures, it will even more important for regional leaders to collaborate and develop a 'regional voice' that can articulate regional needs and seek out new sources of funding and support. The UK Spending Review is a case in point, because without the regional voice being articulated in central government, the North East region will fall even further behind other English regions. In the not too distant past, during the failed 2004 Regional Devolution process there was a combined regional voice emanating from business, local authority, community and voluntary and other civic stakeholders, but now we see a fragmented and patchwork quilt of governance arrangements across the region. In Tees Valley there is a Conservative Mayor, in Middlesbrough an Independent Mayor, and North of Tyne recently appointed a Labour Mayor. Added to these governance arrangements, continuing disputes in between the territories between the Tyne and Tees rivers leave an uncertain future with no resolution to the governance of South of the Tyne. Fragmentation will need to be overcome and national and international experience and best practices are more important than ever.

NOTE

1. *BRIICS* is the term used by the OECD – Brazil, Russia, India, Indonesia, China and South Africa.

GLOSSARY OF ACRONYMS

A&E	Accident and Emergency
APPG	All Party Parliamentary Group
BEIS	Department for Business, Energy and Industrial Strategy
BREXIT	Britain's exit from the European Union
BRICS	Brazil, Russia, India, China, South Africa
BRIICS	Brazil, Russia, India, Indonesia, China, South Africa– emerging countries
BSA	Business Support Activities
CA	Combined Authorities
CCG	Clinical Commissioning Group
DCMS	Department for Digital, Culture, Media and Sport
DEEU	Department for Exiting the European Union
DEFRA	Department for Environment, Food and Rural Affairs
DIT	Department of International Trade
DOT	Department for Transport
ERDF	European Regional Development Fund
ESF	European Social Fund
ESIF	European Structural Investment Fund
EU	European Union
FDI	Foreign Direct Investment

GEOTN	Great Exhibition of the North
GMCA	Greater Manchester Combined Authority
GOR	Government Offices for Regions (abolished 2010)
GP	General Practice
HMT	Her Majesty's Treasury
IDBT	Information, Diagnostic, Brokerage and Transactional Model
ISBE	Institute for Small Business and Enterprise
LEI	Local Economic Initiatives
LEPs	Local Enterprise Partnerships
LGA	Local Government Association
LIS	Local Industrial Strategy
MERG	The Midlands Engine
MHCLG	Department Housing, Communities and Local Government
NELEP	North East Local Enterprise Partnership
NHS	National Health Service
NICE	National Institute for Clinical Excellence
NP	Northern Powerhouse
NPR	Northern Powerhouse Rail
NTCA	North of Tyne Combined Authority
OECD	Organisation for Economic Cooperation and Development
ONS	Office for National Statistics
RAs	Regional Assemblies
R&D	Research and Development
RDA	Regional Development Agency
REF	Research Exercise Framework
RIS	Regional Innovation Strategies (abolished in 2002)

RIS3	Research and Innovation Strategies for Smart Specialisation
RITTS	Regional Innovation and Technology Transfer Strategies
RSA	Regional Studies Association
SME	Small and Medium-sized Enterprises
SIPF	Strength in Places Fund
SPF	Shared Prosperity Fund
TfN	Transport for the North
TSB	Technology Strategy Board
WYCA	West Yorkshire Combined Authority

BIBLIOGRAPHY

Abbasi, M., Cullen, J., Li, C., Molinari, F., Morelli, N., ...,
Van Dam, K. (2019). A triplet under focus: Innovation,
design and the city. In T. I. Concilio (Ed.), *Innovation
capacity and the city. Springer briefs in applied sciences and
technology* (pp. 15–41). Cambridge: Springer.

Adams, R. (2016, September 26). UK universities draw up plans
for EU campuses ahead of Brexit. *The Guardian*. Retrieved
from https://www.theguardian.com/education/2016/sep/22/
ukuniversities-mull-eu-campuses-in-new-era-of-uncertainty

Adams, S. (2005). Stanford and silicon valley: Lessons
on becoming a high-tech region. *California Management
Review*, 48(1), 29–51. doi:10.2307/41166326

Aldrich, H., & Herker, D. (1977). Boundary spanning roles
and organization structure. *The Academy of Management
Review*, 2(2), 217–230.

Allen, T. (2014). *From analysis to action: Connecting
research and local government in an age of Austerity*.
London: Local Government Association.

Allen, T., Grace, C., & Martin, S. (2014). From Analysis to
Action. Connecting Research and Local Government in an
Age of Austerity. Report of the ESRC Local Government
Navigator Programme. London. Local Government
Association.

Amin, A., & Roberts, J. (2008). Knowing in action: Beyond communities of practice. *Research Policy*, 37, 353–369.

Association of North East Councils (ANEC). (2013). *Borderlands: Can the North East and Cumbria benefit from greater Scottish autonomy?* Newcastle: Association of North East Councils. Retrieved from http://www.northeastcouncils. gov.uk/curo/downloaddoc.asp?id=589

Ayres, S., & Beer, A. (2018, November 14). After Brexit, the case for more powerful local government in England will become stronger than ever. *City Metric*. Retrieved from https://www.citymetric.com/fabric/after-brexit-case-more-powerful-local-government-england-will-become-stronger-ever-4344

Baird, B., & McKenna, H. (2019). *Brexit: The implications for health and social care*. London: The King's Fund.

Balconi, M., & Laboranti, A. (2006). University–industry interactions in applied research: The case of microelectronics. *Research Policy*, 35(10), 1616–1630.

Balogun, J., Gleadle, P., Hailey, V. H., & Willmott, H. (2005). Managing change across boundaries: Boundary-shaking practices. *British Journal of Management*, 16, 261–278.

Bambra, C. L., Munford, L., Brown, H., Wilding, A., Robinson, T., Holland, P., …, Sutton, M. (2018). *Health for wealth: Building a healthier northern powerhouse for UK productivity*. Newcastle: Northern Health Sciences Alliance.

BBC. (2019, March 20). What next for the Borderlands' £345m? Retrieved from https://www.bbc.co.uk/news/uk-scotland-south-scotland-47626744

BEIS (Department for Business, Energy and Industrial Strategy). (2016). Science and Innovation Audits: Call

for Expressions of Interest, BEIS, London. https://assets.
publishing.service.gov.uk/government/uploads/system/
uploads/attachment_data/file/570729/beis-16-46-science-
innovation-audits-expressions-of-interest.pdf

Bell, R., Glinianaia, S. V., & Waal, Z. V. (2018). Evaluation
of a complex healthcare intervention to increase smoking
cessation in pregnant women: Interrupted time series
analysis with economic evaluation. *BMJ Tobacco Control*,
27, 90–98.

Bennett, R. J. (2008). SME policy support in Britain since
the 1990s: What have we learnt? *Environment and Planning
C: Government and Policy*, *26*(2), 375–397.

Bentley, G., Pugalis, L., & Shutt, J. (2017). Leadership and
systems of governance: The constraints on the scope for
leadership of place-based development in sub-national
developments. *Regional Studies*, *51*(1), 194–209.

Billing, C., McCann, P., & Ortega-Argiles, R. (2019).
Interregional inequalities and UK sub-national governance
responses to Brexit. *Regional Studies*, *53*(5), 741–760.
doi:10.1080/00343404.2018.1554246

BIS. (2010). *Local growth: Realising every place's potential.*
Department for Business, Innovation and Skills Cm.
7961.London: HMSO.

BIS. (2013). *SMEs: The key enablers of business success and
the economic rationale for government intervention.* Basel,
Switzerland: BIS.

BIS. (2016). *Success as a knowledge economy: Teaching
excellence, social mobility and student choice, success as a
knowledge economy: Teaching excellence, social mobility
and student choice.* London: Department of Education.

Blick, A. (2019). *The two unions: Brexit and the territorial state*. London: The Federal State. Retrieved from https://fedtrust.co.uk/wp-content/uploads/2019/02/The-Two-Unions-Brexit-and-Territorial-State.pdf

Boardman, P. C. (2009). Government centrality to university-industry interactions: university research centers and the industry involvement of academic researchers. *Research Policy*, *38*, 1501–1516.

Borchert, I., & Temberi, N. (2018). *Brexit and regional services: A heat map approach*. The UK Trade Policy Observatory. London: Sussex University and Chatham House, the Royal Institute of International Affairs. Retrieved from http://www.blogs.sussex.ac.uk/uktpo/files/2018/01/briefing-paper-14-heatmap-final.pdf

Boxall, M. (2016, June 28). How can universities prepare for a post-Brexit world? *The Guardian*. Retrieved, from https://www.theguardian.com/higher-education-network/2016/jun/28/how-can-universities-prepare-for-a-post-brexit-world. Accessed on July 29, 2019.

Brandsen, T., Verschuere, B., & Steen, T. (Eds.). (2018). *Co-production and co-creation engaging citizens in public services*. New York, NY: Routledge.

Brien, P. (2019, May 8). *The UK shared prosperity fund*. London: House of Commons.

British Academy. (2017). *Governing England:Devolution and Mayors in England*. Regional Roundtables. Retrieved from https://www.thebritishacademy.ac.uk/sites/default/files/Devolution%20and%20mayors%20in%20England.pdf

Bromley-Davenport, H., MacLeavy, J., & Manley, D. (2018). Brexit in Sunderland: The production of

difference and division in the UK referendum on
European Union membership. *Environment and Planning
C: Politics and Space*. Retrieved from https://doi.
org/10.1177/0263774X18804225

Bulpitt, J. (1983). *Territory and power in the United Kingdom:
An interpretation*. Manchester: Manchester University Press.

Burnham, A. (2019, May 8). London-centric decision-making
led to Brexit. *The Guardian*.

Cabinet Office; Deputy Prime Minister's Office. (2013,
July 5). *City deals*. Retrieved from https://www.gov.uk/
government/collections/city-deals

Cabras, I., Mulvey, G., Shaw, K., Peck, F., & Danson, M.
(2018). *Brexit and the North: The implication of Brexit
for the Northern England and the Anglo-Scottish Border*.
Report for the UK in a Changing Europe. ESRC, London.

Cabras, I., Shaw, K., Danson, M., Peck, F., & Mulvey, G.
(2017). *The implications of Brexit for economic development
and devolved governance in the North of England*. Newcastle
upon Tyne: Newcastle Business School, Northumbria
University. Retrieved from https://www.northumbria.ac.uk/
about-us/academic-departments/newcastle-business-school/
nbs-research/uk-in-a-changing-europe/

Chamber of British Industries. (2018). *How businesses are
preparing for BREXIT 2018*. London: CBI. Retrieved from
http://www.cbi.org.uk/cbi-prod-assets-File/FINAL-brexit-
preparedness-survey-writeup.pdf

Charles, D. (2003). Universities and Territorial
Development: Reshaping the Regional Role of UK
Universities. *Local Economy*, *18*(1), 7–20. doi:https://doi.
org/10.1080/0269094032000073780

Charles, D., & Michie, R. (2013). *Evaluationof the main achievements of cohesion policy programmes and projects over the longer term in 15 selected regions: Case study North East England*. Brussels: European Commission.

Charles, D., Nauwelaers, C., Mouton, B., & Bradley, D. (2000). *Assessment of the regional innovation and technology transfer strategies and infrastructures (RITTS) scheme*. Newcastle upon Tyne: Newcastle University.

Charles, D., Perry, B., & Benneworth, P. (2004). *Towards a multi-level science policy: Regional science policy in a European context*. Sleaford: Regional Studies Association.

Charles, D., & Wray, F. (2015). The English science cities: a new phase in sciense based urban strategy. *International Journal of Knowledge Based Organisations, 5*(1), 46–61.

Chen, W., Los, B., McCann, P., Ortega-Argiles, R., Thissen, M., & van Oort, F. (2018). The continental divide? Economic exposure to BREXIT in regions and countries on both sides of the channel. *Regional Science, 97*(1), 25–54. doi:10.111/pirs.12334

Cherns, A. (1987). Principles of sociotechnical design revisited. *Human Relations, 40*(3), 153.

Chesbrough, H. (2006). *Open business models: How to thrive in the new innovation landscape*. Boston, MA: Harvard Business School Press.

Clark, B. (1989). The academic life: Small worlds, different worlds. *Educational Researcher, 18*(5), 4–8.

Clark, B. R. (1983). The contradictions of change in academic systems (1). *Higher Education, 12*(1), 101–116.

Coaffee, J., & Headlam, N. (2008). Pragmatic localism uncovered: The search for locally contingent solutions to national reform agendas. *Geoforum, 39*(4), 1585–1599. https://doi.org/10.1016/j.geoforum,2007.06.010

Colledge, B. (2015). Anchoring the Northern Powerhouse: Understanding anchor institutions and their contribution within a complex urban and regional system. *Conference proceedings of the Regional Studies Association winter conference*, November (pp. 54–63).

Conrad, M. (2019, July 4). Confidence collapses amid statutory services meltdown. *Municipal Journal,* 1.

Corbett, A. (2016, September 21). *But we can't do it alone: The future of British universities post-Brexit.* London School of Economics. Retrieved from http://blogs.lse.ac.uk/brexit/2016/09/21/but-we-cant-do-it-alone-the-future-of-british-universitiespost-brexit/

Cowie, P., Mulvey, G., Peck, F., & Shaw, K. (2018). *Brexit: Implications for the rural north of England.* ILG. Retrieved from https://www.ncl.ac.uk/media/wwwnclacuk/centreforruraleconomy/files/researchreports/brexitruralnorth-report.pdf

Cox, E. (2017). *Taking back control in the North: A council of the North and other ideas.* Manchester: IPPR North. Retrieved from https://www.ippr.org/files/publications/pdf/taking-back-control-in-the-North_Mar2017.pdf

Cumming, D. J., & Fischer, E. (2012). Publicly funded business advisory services and entrepreneurial outcomes. *Research Policy, 41*(2), 467–481.

Cunningham, J. A., Guerrero, M., Urbano, D. (2017). Entrepreneurial universities: Overview, reflections, and future research agendas. In J. A. Cunningham, M. Guerrero, D. Urbano, (Eds.), *The world scientific reference on entrepreneurship* (Vols. 1: Entrepreneurial Universities - Technology and Knowledge Transfer, pp. 3–19). New York, NY: University at Albany, SUNY.

Cunningham, J. A., & Guerrero, M. (2017). Entrepreneurial universities: Overview, reflections, and future research agendas. In J. A. Cunningham, M. Guerrero, D. Urbano, & D. Siegel (Eds.), *The world scientific reference on entrepreneurship* (Vols. 1: Entrepreneurial Universities – Technology and Knowledge Transfer, pp. 3–19). New York, NY: University at Albany, SUNY.

Cunningham, J. A., Lehmann, E. E., Menter, M., & Seitz, N. (2019). The impact of university focused technology transfer policies on regional innovation and entrepreneurship. *The Journal of Technology Transfer*, 1–25.

Cunningham, J. A., & Link, A. N. (2015). Fostering university-industry R&D collaborations in European Union countries. *International Entrepreneurship and Management Journal*, *11*(4), 849–860.

Curran, J. (2000). What is small business policy in the UK for? Evaluation and assessing small business policies. *International Small Business Journal*, *18*(3), 36–50.

DBIS. (2016). *Success as a Knowledge Economy: Teaching Excellence, Social Mobility and Student Choice.* Cm9258. Department for Business, Innovation and Skills. Available at https://www.gov.uk/government/publications/higher-education-success-as-a-knowledge-economy-white-paper. Accessed on 25 August 2019.

DCMS. (2016). *2016 Creative industries: Focus on employment.* HMSO, London.

DCMS. (2018). *The potential impact of Brexit on the creative industries, tourism and the digital single market: Government response to the Committee's second report of session 2017–19*. London: House of Commons.

Department for Business, Energy and Industrial Strategy. (2015, November 9). *Business Secretary sharpens the UK's innovation expertise with regional research and development audit*. BEIS. Retrieved from https://www.gov.uk/government/news/business-secretary-sharpens-the-uks-innovation-expertise-with-regional-research-and-development-audit

Department for Business, Energy and Industrial Strategy. (2017). *Industrial strategy: Building a Britain fit for the future*. London: BEIS.

Department for Culture, Media and Sport (DCMS). (2016). *2016 Creative industries: Focus on employment*.

Department of Health and Social Care. (2018, October 17). *The future of healthcare: Our vision for digital, data and technology in healthcare*. Retrieved https://www.gov.uk/government/publications/the-future-of-healthcare-our-vision-for-digital-data-and-technology-in-health-and-care/the-future-of-healthcare-our-vision-for-digital-data-and-technology-in-health-and-care. Accessed on July 2019.

Department for Innovation, Universities and Skills. (2008, March). *Innovation nation*. Department for Innovation, Universities and Skills. Retrieved from https://www.gov.uk/government/uploads/system/uploads/attachment_data/file/238751/7345.pdf. Accessed on July 2019.

D'Este, P., & Patel, P. (2007). University–industry linkages in the UK: What are the factors underlying the variety of interactions with industry? *Research Policy*, *36*(9), 1295–1313.

DHCLG. (2018, November 8). North of Tyne combined authority devolution deal. Retrieved from https://www.gov.uk/government/publications/north-of-tyne-combined-authority-devolution-deal. Accessed on July 2019.

Dhingra, S., Machin, S., & Overman, H. (2017). Local economic effects of Brexit. *National Institute Economic Review, 242*(1), R24–R36. doi:https://doi.org/10.1177/002795011724200112

Dickinson, S., & Cox, E. (2016). *Brexit North: Securing a united voice at the negotiating table*. IPPR North. Retrieved from https://www.ippr.org/files/publications/pdf/Brexit-North_Oct2016.pdf. Accessed on July 24, 2019.

Dill, D. D. (2007). Will market competition assure academic quality? An analysis of the UK and US experience. *Quality Assurance in Higher Education*, 47–72.

Dolan, B., Cunningham, J. A., Menter, M., & McGregor, C. (2019). The role and function of cooperative research centers in entrepreneurial universities: A micro level perspective. *Management Decision*.

Dorling, D., Stuart, B., & Stubbs, J. (2016). Don't mention this around the Christmas table: Brexit, inequality and the demographic divide. LSE European Politics and Policy (EUROPP) Blog (21 Dec 2016). Retrieved from http://blogs.lse.ac.uk/europpblog/2016/12/21/christmas-table-brexit-inequality-demographic-divide/

Due North: Report of the enquiry on Health Equity for the North – PHE Response.(2015). PHE Publications Gateway Number 2015025. Retrieved from https://www.gov.uk/government/publications/due-north-report-phe-response

Easterling, K. (2014). Extrastatecraft: the power of infrastructure space. London Verso. Retrieved from https://architecture.mit.edu/history-theory-and-criticism/lecture/extrastatecraft

Edensor, T. (2000). Staging tourism: Tourists as performers. *Annals of Tourism Research, 27*, 322–344.

Eisenschitz, A., & Gough, J. (1998). Theorising the state in local economic governance. *Regional Studies, 32*, 759–768.

Elliott, L. (2017, November 16). No wonder the north is angry. Here's a plan to bridge the bitter Brexit divide. *The Guardian*. Retrieved from https://www.theguardian.com/commentisfree/2017/nov/16/anger-north-brexit-vision-bridge-north-south-divide. Accessed on July 2019.

Empson, W. (2004). *Seven types of ambiguity*. London: Pimlico.

Erno-Kjolhed, K., Husted, K., Monsted, M., & Wenneberg, S. B. (2001, February). Managing university research in the triple helix. *Science and Public Policy, 28*(1), 49–55.

Erturk, I., Froud, J., Johal, S., Leaver, A., & Willliams, K. (2012). Accounting for national success and failure: Rethinking the UK case. *Accounting Forum, 36*(1), 5–17. doi:10.1016/j.accfor.2012.01.004

Etzkowitz, H., & Leydesdorff, L. (2000). The dynamics of innovation: From national systems and "mode 2" to a triple helix of university-industry-government relations. *Research Policy, 29*(2), 109–123.

Federation of Small Businesses. (2018). *Spotlight on innovation: How government can unlock small business productivity*. London: Federation of Small Businesses.

Fenwick, J. (2015). The problem of sub-national governance in England. *Public Money and Management*, *35*(1), 7–14. doi:10.1080/09540962.2015.986859

Fenwick, J., & Elcock, H. (2018). Devolution and federalism in England. *Public Money and Management*, *38*(3), 175–184. doi:10.1080/09540962.2018.1434335

Fielder, R., & Addie, J. P. (2008). *Canadian cities on the edge: Re-assessing the Canadian suburb*. Occasional Papers Volume 1, City of the Institute of York University, Canada.

Flockhart, A. (2019, February 6). Dorset's achievement in a world transformed. Retrieved from https://www.themj.co.uk/Dorsets-achievement-in-a-world-transformed/212875

Florida, R. (2002). *The Rise of the Creative Class*. New York, NY: Basic Book.

Flyberg, B. (2017). *The Oxford handbook of Mega Project Management*. Oxford: Oxford University Press.

FSB. (2018). *Spotlight on innovation: How government can unlock small business productivity*. The Federation of small Business Report, Blackpool, UK.

Garratt, B. (2001). *The Learning Organisation*. London: Harper Collins.

George, G., Zahra, S. A., & Wood, D. R., Jr. (2002). The effects of business–university alliances on innovative output and financial performance: a study of publicly traded biotechnology companies. *Journal of Business Venturing*, *17*(6), 577–609.

Gertner, D., Roberts, J., & Charles, D. (2011). University-industry collaboration: a CoPs approach to KTPs. *Journal of knowledge management*, *15*(4), 625–647.

Geuna, A., & Martin, B. R. (2003). University research evaluation and funding: An international comparison. *Minerva, 41*(4), 277–304.

Giovanni, A. (2016). Towards a 'New English Regionalism' in the North? The case of Yorkshire First. *The Political Quarterly, 87*, 590–600. doi:10.1111/1467-923X.12279

Glasson, J. (2003). The widening local and regional development impacts of the modern universities: A tale of two cities (and North–South perspectives). *Local Economy, 18*(1), 21–37. doi:10.1080/0269094032000073799

Goddard, J., Coombes, M., Kempton, L., & Vallance, P. (2014). Universities as anchor institutions in cities in a turbulent funding environment: Vulnerable institutions and vulnerable places in England. *Cambridge Journal of Regions, Economy and Society, 7*(2), 307–325. doi:https://doi.org/10.1093/cjres/rsu004

Goddard, J., Hazelkorn, E., Kempton, L., & Vallance, P. (2016). *The civic university*. Cheltenham: Edward Elgar.

Goddard, J., & Tewdwr-Jones, M. (2016). *Civic universities and the civic university*. Newcastle: Newcastle University.

Goodwin, M. J., & Heath, O. (2016). The 2016 referendum, Brexit and the left behind: An aggregate-level analysis of the result. *The Political Quarterly, 87*, 323–332. doi:10.1111/1467-923X.12285

GOV.UK. (2016). *Making IT work: Harnessing the power of health information*. Retrieved from https://www.gov.uk/government/publications/using-information-technology-to-improve-the-nhs

GOV. UK. (2018a). The future of healthcare: Our vision for digital, data and technology in health and care. Retrieved from https://www.gov.uk/government/publications/the-future-of-healthcare-our-vision-for-digital-data-and-technology-in-health-and-care/the-future-of-healthcare-our-vision-for-digital-data-and-technology-in-health-and-care

GOV.UK. (2018b). EU settlement scheme. Retrieved from https://www.gov.uk/settled-status-eu-citizens-families/applying-for-settled-status?utm_campaign=EU SS&utm_medium=paid_search&utm_source=Google&gclid=EAIaIQobChMIj9PW95Wt4wIVCLLtCh0pHgiS EAAYASAAEgIlGfD_BwE&gclsrc=aw.ds

GOV.UK. (2019, July 1). Boost for borderlands: Growth deal signed. Retrieved from https://www.gov.uk/governme nt/news/boost-for-borderlands-growth-deal-signed. Accessed on July 2019.

Headlam, N. (2011). Greater Manchester city region, culminating its designation as a Statutory City-Regional Pilot [SCR] from 2010/11. Manchester: Work in Progress. Governance Networks for Economic Development in the Greater Manchester City Region.

Greene, F., Mole, K., & Storey, D. (2008). *Three decades of enterprise culture*. Basingstoke: Palgrave.

Grint, K. (2010). *Leadership: A very short introduction*. Oxford: Oxford University Press.

Guerrero, M., Cunningham, J. A., & Urbano, D. (2015). Economic impact of entrepreneurial universities' activities: An exploratory study of the United Kingdom. *Research Policy, 41*(4), 748–764.

Guerrero, M., Urbano, D., Cunningham, J., & Organ, D. (2014). Entrepreneurial universities in two European regions: A case study comparison. *The Journal of Technology Transfer*, *39*(3), 415–434.

Hambleton, R., & Sweeting, D. (2015). *The impact of Mayoral governance in Bristol*. Bristol: University of Bristol.

Hanson, D. (1983). *The new Alchemists: Silicon valley and the microelectronics revolution*. New York, NY: Avon Books. doi:ISBN0380658542 (ISBN13: 9780380658541)

Harris, R., & Charlton, M. (2016). Voting out of the European Union: Exploring the geography of leave. *Environment and Planning A: Economy and Space*, *48*(11), 2116–2128. doi:https://doi.org/10.1177/0308518X16665844

Harvey, D. (1989). *The condition of postmodernity: An enquiry into the origins of cultural change*. Oxford: Blackwell.

Haughton, G., & Allmendinger, P. (2013). Spaces of neo-liberal experimentation: Soft spaces, post politics and neo-liberal governmentality. *Environment and Planning A: Economics and Space*, *45*(1), 2013. https://doi.org/10.1068/a45121

Hayter, C. S., Link, A. N., & Scott, J. T. (2018). Public-sector entrepreneurship. *Oxford Review of Economic Policy*, *34*(4), 676–694.

Headlam, N., Healey, P. (2006). Transforming governance: Challenges of institutional adaptation and a new politics of space. *European Planning Studies*, *14*(3), 299–320.

HEPI. (2018). The costs and benefits of international student by parliamentary constituency. *Retrieved from* https://www.hepi.ac.uk/wp-content/uploads/2018/01/Economic-benefits-

of-international-students-by-constituency-Final-11-01-2018.
pdf. Accessed on June 29, 2019.

HESA. (2017). *Students in higher education 2015/16*, Higher
Education Statistics Authority, London.

Heseltine, M. (2012). *No stone unturned: In pursuit of
growth*. London: Department for Business Innovation and
Skills.

Heseltine, M. (2019). *Empowering English cities. English
Mayoral combined authorities*. London: Haymarket
Group. Retrieved from https://englishcitiesmichaelheseltine.
premediastudio.com/MichaelHeseltine/. Accessed on July
2019.

Hesse, B. (2018). Can psychology walk the walk of open
science? *American Psychologist, 73*(2), 126.

Hoare, T. (1991). University competition, student migration
and regional economic differentials in the United Kingdom.
Higher Education, 22(4), 351–370.

Horst, W., Rittel, M., & Webber, M. (1973). *Dilemmas
in a general theory of planning* (p. 160). Berkeley, CA:
Institute of Urban and Regional Development, University of
California.

House of Commons. (2015). *Combined authorities*. London:
House of Commons.

House of Commons. (2019a). *Brexit and local government*.
London: Housing Communities and Local Government
Committee. Retrieved, from https://publications.parliament.
uk/pa/cm201719/cmselect/cmcomloc/493/493.pdf. Accessed
on July 2019.

House of Commons. (2019b). *Exiting the EU*. Higher
Education Report. Retrieved from https://www.parliament.

uk/documents/commons-committees/Exiting-the-European-Union/17-19/Sectoral%20Analyses/19-Higher-Education-Report.pdf. Accessed on July 1, 2019.

House of Commons. (2019d). Higher Education Report, House of Commons Exiting the European Union, https://www.parliament.uk/documents/commons-committees/Exiting-the-European-Union/17-19/Sectoral%20Analyses/19-Higher-Education-Report.pdf. Accessed on 1st July 2019.

Hudson, R., & Williams, A. (1995). *Divided Britain* (2nd ed.). Chichester: John Wiley & Sons.

Hutton, W. (2018, February 18). You've heard about the north–south divide. How about the east–west one? *The Guardian*.

Health Education England (2019, February). The Topol review. Preparing the healthcare workforce to deliver the digital future. (2019). Retrieved from https://www.hee.nhs.uk/our-work/topol-review. Accessed in July 2019.

IPPR North. (2017). *Forgotten opportunities: The dynamic role of the rural economy in post-Brexit Britain*. Manchester: Institute for Public Policy Research. Retrieved from https://www.ippr.org/files/publications/pdf/forgotten-opportunities-feb2017.pdf

IPPR North. (2019). *SMEs and productivity in the Northern Powerhouse*. Manchester: IPPR.

Jagger, C. (2015). *Trends in life expectancy and healthy life expectancy. The future of an aging population project: Evidence review*. London: NHS.

Jeffery, C., Wyn Jones, R., Henderson, A., Scully, R., & Lodge, G. (2014). *Taking England seriously: The New*

English politics. London: ESRC Scottish Centre on Constitutional Change.

Jennings, W., Stoker, G., & Warren, I. (2019). *Brexit and public opinion: Cities and towns – The geography of discontent*. ESRC. Retrieved from https://ukandeu.ac.uk/brexit-and-public-opinion-cities-and-towns-the-geography-of-discontent/

Jessop, B., Bonnett, K., Bromley, S., & Ling, T. (1988). *Thatcherism: A tale of two nations*. Cambridge: Polity.

Johnson, D. (2015a). Tackling Britain's regional inequalities. In Union21, *Rebalancing The Economy: New thinking on Britain's regional inequalities*. London: Union 21. Retrieved from http://unions21.org.uk/files1/UNIONS21_24809_proofC.pdf. Accessed on June 26, 2019.

Johnson, D. (2015b, March 20). It's regional inequality, stupid. *New Statesman*. Retrieved from https://www. newstatesman.com/politics/2015/03/its-regional- inequality-stupid

Johnson, J. (2019, May 29). Available at https://twitter.com/jojohnsonuk/status/1133773288579260416. Accessed 26 August 2019.

Jones, R. (2018, Winter). The second coming of industrial strategy. *Issues in Science and Technology*, 34(2), 59–65.

Jones, R., & Sabbagh, D. (2019, February 3). Nissan warns of BREXIT concerns as U-turn at Sunderland confirmed. *The Guardian*. Retrieved from https://www.theguargian.com/business/2019/feb/03/nissan-confirms-new-x-trail-will-not-be-built-in-sunderland

Kealy, D. (2016). A tale of one city: The Devo Manc deal and its implications for English devolution. *The Political Quarterly*, 87. doi:10.1111/1467-923X.12278

Kenealy, D. (2016). A Tale of One City: The Devo Manc Deal and Its Implications for English Devolution. *The Political Quarterly, 87,*572–581. doi:10.1111/1467-923X.12278.

Kerslake, B. (2019, May). *Fairer and stronger: Rebalancing the UK economy.* Sheffield: Sheffield University.

Knight, C. L. (2013). Knowledge brokers: The role of intermediiaries in producing research impact. *Evidence and Policy, 9*(3), 309–916.

Knight, C. & Lyall, C. (2013). Knowledge brokers: the role of intermediaries in producing research impact. *Evidence and Policy, 9*(3), 309–316.

Kooiman, J. (2003). *Governing as governance.* London: Sage.

Korhonena, J. N. (2018, February 20). Circular economy as an essentially contested concept. *Journal of Cleaner Production, 175,* 544–552.

Leach, S., Stewart, J., & Jones, G. (2018). *Centralisation, devolution and the future of local government in England.* London: Routledge.

Lee, S., & Bozeman, B. (2005). The Impact of Research Collaboration on Scientific Productivity. *Social Studies of Science, 35*(5), 673–702.

Lee, Y. (2000). The sustainability of university–industry research collaboration: An empirical assessment. *The Journal of Technology Transfer, 25*(2), 111–133.

Lewis, J., & Townsend, A. (1989). Introduction: The emergence of an issue. In J. Lewis & A. Townsend (Eds.), *The North–South divide* (pp. 20–60). London: Chapman.

Leyden, D. P., & Link, A. N. (2015). *Public sector entrepreneurship: US technology and innovation policy.* Oxford: Oxford University Press.

Liddle, J., & Shutt, J. (2019). *The North East after Brexit: Impact and Policy*. Bingley: Emerald Publishing.

Lloyd, C. (2018, December 4). Done deal: Mayor bids £40m to buy airport. *The Northern Echo*. Retrieved from https://www.thenorthernecho.co.uk/news/17275632.done-deal-mayor-bids-40m-to-buy-airport/. Accessed on July 2019.

Los, B., McCAnn, P., Springford, J., & Thissen, M. (2017). The mismatch between local voting and the local economic consequences of Brexit. *Regional Studies*, *51*(5), 786–799. doi:10.1080/00343404.2017.1287350

Lowther, J. (2015). SOLACE Research Brief. *ESRC Knowledge Navigator Programme*.

MacCannell, D. (1973). Staged authenticity: arrangements of social space in tourist settings. *American Sociological Review*, *79*, 589–603.

MacCannell, D. (1976). *The tourist: A new theory of the leisure class*. New York, NY: Sulouker.

MacDonald, R. (2017). "Impact", research and slaying Zombies: The pressures and possibilities of the REF. *International Journal of Sociology and Social Policy*, *37*(11–12), 696–710.

MacKay, B. (2016). *How might Brexit impact on Britain's universities* . Centre for Constitutional Change. Retrieved from http://www.centreonconstitutionalchange.ac.uk/blog/how-might-brexit-impactbritain%E2%80%99s-universities

MacLeod, G., & Jones, M. (2018). Explaining 'Brexit capital': Uneven development and the austerity state. *Space and Polity*, *22*(2), 111–136. doi:10.1080/13562576.2018.1535272

MacNamara, O. (2012). *Urban regeneration making a difference*. London: Higher Education Funding Council for Great Britain.

Maitland, R. (2013). Backstage behaviour in the global city: Tourists and the search for the 'real London'. *Procedia-Social and Behavioural Sciences*, *105*(6), 12–19.

Marginson, S. (2017). Brexit: Challenges for universities in hard times. *International Higher Education*, *88*, 8–10. doi:https://doi.org/10.6017/ihe.2017.88.9682

Marlow, D. (2015, April 28). Making the university 'anchor institution' a reality towards more purposeful local government-university relations. *London: Local Government Information Unit Briefing*.

Marques, J. P., Caraca, J. M., & Diz, H. (2006). How can university–industry–government interactions change the innovation scenario in Portugal? The case of the University of Coimbra. *Technovation*, *26*(4), 534, 542.

Martin, R., Pike, A., Tyler, P., & Gardiner, B. (2016). Spatially rebalancing the UK economy: Towards a New policy model? *Regional Studies*, *50*(2), 342–357.

Mason, C., & Brown, R. (2014). *Entrepreneurial ecosystems and growth orientated entrepreneurship: The Hague, Netherlands*. The Hague, Netherlands: OECD.

Mawson, J. (2007). Research Councils, Universities and Local Government: Building Bridges. *Public Policy and Management*, *24*(4), 265–273.

Mawson, J. (2009). *A unique venture in the North East. Institute for local governance*. Durham, NC: The Institute for Local Governance, Durham University.

Mawson, J. (2009a). *A unique venture in the North East. Institute for Local Governance.* Durham: The Institute for Local Governance, Durham University.

Mawson, J. (2009b). 'How research can break down the barriers'. Local Government Chronicle, 15.10.2009.

Mawson, J. (2011). *Issues and Challenges at the Research Practice Interface. A Review.* Institute for Local Governance, Durham University.

Mawson, J. (2015). 'University-Local Government Research Collaboration in the North East'. Paper given at ESRC: Society of Local Authority Chief Executives, Local Government Association Conference on *New Routes to Collaboration.* London. 27.03.2015.

Mawson, J. (2019). ILG Research Projects and Seminars 2009–2019. Institute for Local Governance, Durham University.

May, T., Perry, B., Hodson, M., & Marvin, S. (2009). *Active intermediaries for effective knowledge exchange.* Salford: Sustainable Urban and Regional Futures (SURF) University of Salford.

Mayhew, K. (2017). UK Higher Education and Brexit, *Oxford Review of Economic Policy*, *33*(S1), S155–S161

Mazzucato, M. (2015). *The entrepreneurial state: Debunking public vs. private sector myths.* London: Anthem Press.

McCann, P. (2016). *The UK Regional–National economic problem. Geography, globalisation and governance.* London: Routledge.

McCann, P. (2019, forthcoming). Perceptions of regional inequality and the geography of discontent: Insights from the UK. *Regional Studies*. Retrieved from https://doi.org/10.1080/00343404.2019.1619928

McCann, P., & Ortego-Argiles, R. (2019). *'UK regions' in Article 50; Two years on*. The UK in a changing Europe. Retrieved from https://ukandeu.ac.uk/wp-content/uploads/2019/03/Article-50-two-years-on.pdf

McLoughlin, I., & Wilson, R. (2013). *Digital government at work: A social informatics approach*. Oxford: Oxford University Press.

Menon, A., & Salter, J. P. (2016). Brexit: Initial reflections. *International Affairs*, 92(6), 1297–1318. doi:https://doi.org/10.1111/1468-2346.12745

Meyer-Krahmer, F., & Schmoch, U. (1998). Science-based technologies: University–industry interactions in four fields. *Research Policy*, 27(8), 835–851.

Miller, K., Alexander, A., Cunningham, J. A., & Albats, E. (2018). Entrepreneurial academics and academic entrepreneurs: A systematic literature review. *International Journal of Technology Management*, 77(1/2/3), 9–37.

Mintrom, M., & Norman, P. (2009). Policy entrepreneurship and policy change. *Policy Studies Journal*, 37(4), 649–667. https://doi.org/10.1111/j.1541-0072,2009,00329.x

Mintzberg, H., Lampel, A., & Anisbrand, B. (1998). *Strategy Safari. A Guided tour Through the Wilds of Strategic Management*. Hemel Hempstead: Prentice Hall.

Mitlin, D. (2008). With and beyond the state: Co-production as a route to political influence, power and transformation for grassroots organizations. *Environment and Urbanization*, 20(2), 339–360.

Mole, K. F. (2002). Street-level technocracy in UK small business support: Business links, personal business advisers, and the small business service. *Environment and Planning C: Government and Policy*, *20*, 179–194.

Mole, K. F., & Bramley, G. (2006). Making policy choices in nonfinancial business support: An international comparison. *Environment and Planning C: Government and Policy*, *24*(6), 885–908.

Mole, K. F., Hart, M., & Roper, S. (2014). When moving information online diminishes change: Advisory services to SMEs. *Policy Studies*, *35*, 172–191.

Mole, K. F., Hart, M., Roper, S., & Saal, D. (2009). Assessing the effectiveness of business support services in England: Evidence from a theory based evaluation. *International Small Business Journal*, *27*, 557–582.

Mole, K. F., Hart, M., Roper, S., & Saal, D. (2011). Broader or deeper? Exploring the most effective intervention profile for public small business support. *Environment and Planning A*, *43*, 87–105.

Mordue, T. (2005). Tourism, performance and social exclusion in "Olde York". *Annals of Tourism Research*, *32*(1), 179–198.

Mordue, T. (2007). Tourism, urban governance and public space. *Leisure Studies*, *26*(4), 447–462.

Mordue, T. (2017). New urban tourism and new urban citizenship: Researching the creation and management of postmodern urban public space. *International Journal of Tourism Cities*, *3*(4), 399–405.

Moss Kanter, R. (1997). *The imagination to innovate, the professionalism to perform, and the openness to collaborate: Leading the change-adept organisation.* Rosabeth Moss

Kanter on the Frontiers of Management. Brighton, MA: Harvard Business School Press.

Mulgan, G. (2010). *The art of public strategies: Mobilising power and knowledge for the common good.* Oxford: Oxford University Press.

National Audit Office. (2015). *Devolving responsibilities to cities in England: Wave 1 city deals.* London: House of Commons. Retrieved from http://www.nao.org.uk/wp-content/uploads/2015/07/Devolving-responsibilities-to-cities-in-England-Wave-One-City-Deals.pdf

National Audit Office. (2017). *Progress in setting up combined authorities.* London: House of Commons.

National Audit Office (NAO). (2019). *Local enterprise partnerships: An update on progress.* London: NAO.

NECA. (2016). *Health and wealth: Closing the gap in the North East.* Executive Summary of the Report of the North East Commission for Health and Social Care Integration. Retrieved from https://www.ntw.nhs.uk/content/uploads/2017/02/Agenda-item-9-i-c-Executive-Summary-Health-and-Wealth-Closing-the-Gap-in-the-North-East.pdf

NELEP. (2014). *More and better jobs: A strategic economic plan for the North East.* Newcastle upon Tyne: NELEP.

NELEP. (2018a). *North East Brexit Group response. APPG on Post-Brexit funding for nations, regions and local areas.* Newcastle upon Tyne: NELEP.

NELEP. (2018b). Our economy 2018. Retrieved from https://www.nelep.co.uk/wp-content/uploads/2018/03/our-economy-exec-summary-final-lr.pdf. Accessed on June 29, 2019.

NELEP. (2018c). *Our Economy 2018. With insights into global connections*. Newcastle upon Tyne: NELEP. Retrieved from https://www.nelep.co.uk/wp-content/upload/2018/03/nel237a-our-economy-v10-web-full.pdf

NELEP. (2019a, July). Leaving the European union. Retrieved from https://www.northeastlep.co.uk/wp-content/uploads/2018/06/nel377-sector-study-a4-final-version.pdf

NELEP. (2019b). *North East Brexit group: Brexit preparation overview*. Newcastle upon Tyne: NELEP.

NELEP. (2019c). *North East strategic economic plan*. Newcastle upon Tyne: NELEP.

Nelles, J. (2013). Cooperation or capacity? Exploring the limits of city-region governance partnerships. *International Journal of Urban and Regional Research*, 37(4), 1349–1367. https://doi.org//10.111/j.1468-2427.2012.01112.x

Nelson, R. (1993). *National innovation systems: A comparative analysis*. Oxford: Oxford University Press.

NESTA. (2006). *The innovation gap. Why policy needs to reflect the reality of innovation in the UK*. Nesta report. NESTA, London

NHS. (2019e).The NHS long term plan. Retrieved from https://www.longtermplan.nhs.uk/

NHS. (2014). Five year forward view. Retrieved from https://www.england.nhs.uk/wp-content/uploads/2014/10/5yfv-web.pdf. Accessed on July 2019.

NHS. (2016). Making IT work:Harnessing the power of health information technology to improve care in England. Retrieved froms https://www.gov.uk/government/publications/using-information-technology-to-imporove-the-nh. Accessed on July 2019.

NHS. (2018). The future of healthcare: Our vision for digital, data and technology in healthcare. Retrieved https:/www.gov.uk/government/publications/the-future-of-healthcare-our-vision-for-digital-data-and-technology-in-health-and-care. Accessed on July 2019.

NHS. (2019a, July). Defining the role of integrated care systems in workforce. Retrieved from https://www.nhsconfed.org/resources/2019/03/defining-the-role-of-integrated-care-systems-in-workforce-development. Accessed on July 2019.

NHS. (2019b). Global digital exemplars. Retrieved from https://www.england.nhs.uk/digitaltechnology/connecteddigitalsystems/exemplars/

NHS. (2019c). Interim NHS people plan. Retrieved from https://www.longtermplan.nhs.uk/wp-content/uploads/2019/05/Interim-NHS-People-Plan_June2019.pdf. Accessed on July 2019.

NHS. (2019d). NHS Assembly accessed. Retrieved from https://www.longtermplan.nhs.uk/nhs-assembly/. Accessed on July 2019

NHS. (2019e).The NHS long term plan. Retrieved from https://www.longtermplan.nhs.uk/

NHS England. (2016). New care models: Vanguards – Developing a blueprint for the future of NHS and care services. Retrieved from https://www.england.nhs.uk/new-care-models/about/

NHS England. (2018a). Equality and health inequality NHS RightCare packs. Retrieved from https://www.england.nhs.uk/rightcare/products/ccg-data-packs/equality-and-health-inequality-nhs-rightcare-packs/. Accessed on July 2019.

NHS England. (2018b). Equality and health inequality NHS Right Care packs 2018-North. Retrieved from https://www.england.nhs.uk/publication/equality-and-health-inequalities-packs-2018-north/. Accessed on July 2019.

NHS England. (2019a). NHS long term plan. Retrieved from https://www.longtermplan.nhs.uk/

NHS England. (2019b). The Topol review. Preparing the healthcare workforce to deliver the digital future. Retrieved from https://www.hee.nhs.uk/our-work/topol-review. Accessed on July 2019.

NHS England. (2019c). Interim NHS people plan. Retrieved from https://www.longtermplan.nhs.uk/wp-content/uploads/2019/05/InterimNHS-People- Plan_June2019.pdf. Accessed on July 2019.

NHS England. (2019d). NHS Assembly. Retrieved from https://www.longtermplan.nhs.uk/nhs-assembly/

NHS England. (2019e). Integrated Care Systems. Retrieved from https://www.england.nhs.uk/integratedcare/integrated-care-systems/. Accessed on 16 October 2019.

National Institute for Health and Care Excellence (NICE). (2018). Intermediate care including reablement. Retrieved from https://www.nice.org.uk/guidance/qs173. Accessed on July 2019.

NELEP. (2013). The North East Economic Review Report. Available at https://www.nelep.co.uk/wp-content/uploads/2014/11/North-East-Independent-Economic-Review-April2013.pdf

North East Brexit Group. (2018). *Leaving the EU. A review of evidence about opportunities, challenges and risks to the North East economy and its key sectors with recommendations for action*. Newcastle upon Tyne: North East LEP. Retrieved from https://www.nelep.co.uk/wp-content/uploads/2018/06/nel377-sector-study-a4-final-version.pdf. Accessed on July 2019.

North East England Chamber of Commerce. (2018). Quarterly economic survey. Retrieved from https://www.neechamber.co.uk/updates/chamber-news/chamber-economic-survey-q1-shows-strong-export-hyphen-growth

North East LEP. (2013). *North East independent economic review*. Newcastle: NELEP. Retrieved from https://www.nelep.co.uk/wp-content/upload/2014/11/north-East-independent-economic-review-April-2013.pdf

North of Tyne. (2018). *Home of ambition. The vision for the North of Tyne combined authority*. Retrieved from https://static1.squarespace.com/static/5bbf08bdc2ff616708156a58/t/5be323872b6a2815fe9ab467/1541612442072/North+of+Tyne_Economic+Vision_web+final.pdf

Nutley, S., Walter, I., & Davies, T. (2007). *Using evidence. How research can inform public services*. Bristol: Policy Press.

OECD. (2009). *How regions grow: Trends and analysis*. Paris: OECD.

OECD. (2010). *Regions matter*. Paris: OECD.

O'Kane, C., Zhang, J. A., Cunningham, J. A., & O'Reilly, P. (2017). What factors inhibit publicly funded principal investigators' commercialization activities? *Small Enterprise Research*, 24(3), 215–232.

O'Brien, P., & Pike, A. (2015). City deals, decentralisation and the governance of local infrastructure funding and financing in the UK. *National Institute Economic Review*. https://doi.org/10.1177/002795011523300103

O'Kane, C., Zhang, J. A., Daellenbach, U., & Davenport, S. (2019). Building entrepreneurial behaviours in academic scientists: Past perspective and new initiatives. In M. MacAdam & J. A. Cunningham (Eds.), *Entrepreneurial behaviour* (pp. 145–166). London: Macmillan.

O'Neill. (2019). £260m pledged for Borderlands growth deal. *Local Government Chronicle*. Retrieved from https://www.lgcplus.com/politics/devolution-and-economic-growth/260m-pledged-for-borderlands-growth-deal/7028201.article

ONS. (2016). *Regional gross disposable household income (GDHI) at current basic prices*. London: Office for National Statistics.

Osborne, G. (2018, February 1). Osborne urges PM to focus on the North–South divide. *London Evening Standard*.

Ostram, E., & Baugh, W. H. (1973). *Community organization and the provision of police services*. Beverly Hills, CA: Sage Publications.

Paine, D. (2015, February 28). 'Revealed': the 40 years that could form Combined Authorities. Local Government Chronicle

Perkmann, M., & Walsh, K. (2009, June 17–19). The two faces of collaboration: Impacts of university–industry relations on public research. *CBS-Copenhagen business school summer conference*, Copenhagen.

Pestoff, V., & Brandsen, T. (2007). *Co-production: The third sector and the delivery of public services*.London: Routledge.

Pettigrew, A. M. (2001). Management research after modernism. *British Journal of Management, 12,* 62–72.

Pike, A. (2018). Devolution in England needs real powers and resources if it is to 'take back control' in Brexit. Retrieved from https://ukandeu.ac.uk/devolution-in-england-needs-real-powers-and-resources-if-it-is-to-take-back-control-in-brexit/

Pike, A., Kempton, L., Marlow, D., O'Brien, P., & Tomaney, J. (2016). *Decentralisation: Issues, principles and practice.* Newcastle: CURDS, Newcastle University. Retrieved from https://www.ncl.ac.uk/media/wwwnclacuk/curds/files/decentralisation.pdf

Pike, A., O'Brien, P., Strickland, T., Thrower, G., & Tomaney, J. (2019a). Deal or no deal? Austerity, decentralisation and the City Deals. In A. Pike, P. O'Brien, T. Strickland, G. Thrower, & J. Tomaney (Eds.), *Financialising city statecraft and infrastructure.* Cheltenham: Edward Elgar. doi:https://doi.org/10.4337/9781788118958

Pike, A., O'Brien, P., Strickland, T., Thrower, G., & Tomaney, J. (2019b). *Financialising city infrastructure and governance.* London: Edward Elgar. doi:https://doi.org/10.4337/9781788118958

Pike, A., & Tomaney, J. (2009). The state and uneven development: The governance of economic development in England in the post-devolution UK. *Cambridge Journal of the Regions, Economy and Society*, 2(1), 13–34.

Prescott, J. (2018, May 18). Manchester is the London of the North. *Yorkshire Post.*

Public Health England. (2019a). Due North: Report of the inquiry on health equity for the North. Retrieved from https://www.gov.uk/government/publications/due-north-report-phe-response

Public Health England. (2019b). State of the North East 2018: Public health and wellbeing. Retrieved from https://assets.publishing.service.gov.uk/government/uploads/system/uploads/attachment_data/file/779473/state_of_the_north_east_2018_public_mental_health_and_wellbeing.pdf

Public Health England. (2019c). Public health outcomes framework-map. Retrieved from https://fingertips.phe.org.uk/profile/public-health-outcomes-framework/data#page/8/gid/1000049/pat/6/par/E12000001/ati/101/are/E06000057

Public Sector Executive. (2019, May 5). Governmenr agrees to £30m a year South Yorkshire Devolution Deal. Retrieved from http://www.publicsectorexecutive.com/Public-Sector-News/government-agrees-to-30m-a-year-south-yorkshire-devolution-deal

Pugalis, L., & Gray, N. (2016). New regional development paradigms: An exposition of place based modalities. *Australasion Journal of Regional Studies*, *22*(1), 181–201.

PWC. (2018). *Workforce of the future: The competing forces shaping 2030.*

Richard, D. (2008). *Small business and government: The Richard report*. Submission to the Shadow Cabinet. London: Conservative Party.

Richards, G. (2014). Creativity and tourism in the city. *Current Issues in Tourism*, *17*(2), 119–144.

Ritzer, G. (2005). *Enchanting a disenchanted world: Revolutionising the means of consumption*. London: Sage.

Robbins, K. (1991). Tradition and translation: National culture in its global context. In J. Corner & S. Harvey (Eds.),

Enterprise and heritage: Crosscurrents of national culture (pp. 21–44). London: Routledge.

Robinson, F. S. (2000). *Who runs the North East*. Durham: Durham University.

Robinson, F., & Shaw, K. (1994). *Quangos in the North of England*. Durham: Durham University/UNISON.

Robinson, F., Shaw, K., & Hopwood, B. (2000). *Who Runs the North East*. Durham: Durham University.

Robinson, F., Shaw, K., & Regan, S. (2017). *Who runs the North East now? Governance and governing in an English region*. Durham: Northumbria University and St. Chad's College Durham University.

Rodriguez-Pose, A. (2019). The revenge of the places that don't matter (and what to do about it). *Cambridge Journal of Regions, Economy and Society*, *11*, 189–209.

Rogers, E., & Larson, J. (1986). *Silicon Valley fever: Growth of high-technology culture*. New York, NY: HarperCollins Publishers.

Round, A., & Hunter, J. (2019). *Perspectives on SMEs and productivity in the Northern Powerhouse: Final report*. Manchester: IPPR North.

Rushton, P. (2017). *The myth and reality of Brexit City: Sunderland and the 2016 referendum*. University of Sunderland. Retrieved from http://sure.sunderland.ac.uk/id/eprint/9234/

Rusk, M. (2018). Proceedings of the 6th international conference on innovation and entrepreneurship. In D. A. Bedford & E. G. Carayannis (Eds.), *Innovation by design dynamics* (Vol. ICIE 2018, pp. 600–608).

Rusk, M., & McGowan, P. (2015). Entrepreneurial learning in context: An exploration of learning models in different domains. In R. P. Dameri, R. Garelli, & M. Resta (Ed.), *Proceedings of ECIE 2015 10th European conference on innovation and entrepreneurship, Genoa, Italy*. Reading, MA: Academic Conferences and Publishing International Limited.

Russell, M., & Sheldon, J. (2018). *Options for an English Parliament*. The constitution unit: UCL. Retrieved from https://www.ucl.ac.uk/constitution-unit/sites/constitution-unit/files/179-options-for-an-english-parliament.pdf. Accessed on July 2019.

Sacco, P. L. (2011). Culture 3.0: A new perspective for the EU 2014-2020 structural funds programming. EENC Paper, April 2011.

Santander Enterprise Index. (2014) Benchmarking the Regional Ecosystem for Entrepreneurs in the UK. November 2014. DOI: 10.13140/RG.2.1.2848.0168. Santander UK.

Sayer, D. (2014). *Rank hypocrisies: The insult of the REF*. London: Sage.

Schafer, L. (2016). *Performance assessment in science and academia:effects of the RAE/REF on academic life*. CGHE Working Papers.

Scottish Borders Council. (2018). *Borderlands inclusive growth deal: Next steps*. Report by the Executive Director. Retrieved from https://scottishborders.moderngov.co.uk/documents/s31010/Item%20No.%2014%20-%20Borderlands%20Inclusive%20Growth%20Deal%20report.pdf. Accessed on July 2019.

Shaw, K. (2012). The rise of the resilient local authority. *Local Government Studies*, *33*(3), 281–300.

Shaw, K. (2018). "Northern lights:" An assessment of the political and economic challenges facing North East England in the context of greater Scottish autonomy. *Journal of Borderlands Studies*, *33*(1), 35–52.

Shaw, K., Peck, F., Jackson, K., & Mulvey, G. (2015). *Developing the framework for a Borderlands strategy. A report for the Borderlands Stakeholder Group*. Cumbria: Universities of Northumbria and Cumbria.

Shaw, K., & Robinson, F. (2011). Don't mention the "R Word": The end of regionalism in the North East? Town and Country Planning 80(12), 534–538.

Shaw, K., & Robinson, F. (2012). From 'regionalism' to 'localism': Opportunities and challenges for North East England. Local Economy, 27(3), 232–250. https://doi.org/10.1177/0269094211434468

Shaw, K., & Robinson, F. (2018). Whatever happened to the North East? Reflections on the end of Regionalism in England. *Local Economy*, *33*(8), 842–861. doi:https://doi.org/10.1177/0269094218819789

Shaw, K. F., Robinson, F., & Blackie, J. (2014). Borderlands: Rescaling economic development in Northern England in the context of greater Scottish autonomy. *Local Economy*, *29*(4–5), 412–428.

Shaw, K. R. (2011). Don't mention the "R Word": The end of regionalism in the North East? *Town and Country Planning*, *80*(12), 534–538.

Shutt, J., & Liddle, J. (2019a). Are combined authorities in England strategic and fit for purpose? *Local Economy*, *34*(2), 91–93. doi:https://doi.org/10.1177/0269094219839956

Shutt, J., & Liddle, J. (2019b). Combined authorities in England. Moving beyond devolution: Developing strategic local government for a more sustainable future? *Local Economy*, *34*(2), p196–207. doi:https://doi.org/10.1177/0269094219839966

Sivaev, D. (2013). How should we help business grow? Delivering business support. *Local Economy*, *28*, 906–910.

Sotarauta, M., Beer, A., & Gibney, J. (2016). Making sense of leadership in urban and regional development. *Regional Studies*, *51*(2), 187–193.

Staged Authenticity: Arrangements of social place in tourist setting. (1973, January). *American Journal of Sociology*, *79*, 586–603.

Steel, N., Ford, J., Newton, J., Davis, A., Vos, T., & Naghavi, M. (2018). Changes in health in the countries fo the UK and 150 English Local Authority areas 1990–2016: A systematic analysis for the Global Burden of Disease Society 2016. *The Lancet, 392*(10158), 1647–1661. Retrieved from https://www.thelancet.com/journals/lancet/article/PIIS0140-6736(18)32207-4/fulltext

Stephenson, K. (2004) Towards a Theory of Government. In H. McCarthy, P. Miller, & P. Skidmore (Eds.), *Network Logic: who governs in an interconnected world?* (pp. 37–48). London: Demos. Available: http://www.drkaren.us/pdfs/networklogic03stephenson%5B1%5D.pdf. Accessed on 25 March 2011.

Stone, C. N. (2015). Reflections on regime politics: From governing coalition to urban political order. *Urban Affairs Review*, *51*, 101–137. doi:10.1177/1078087414558948

Storey, D. (2003). Entrepreneurship, small and medium sized enterprises and public policies. In Z. J. Acs & D. B. Audretsch (Eds.), *The handbook of Entrepreneurship* (pp. 473–511). London: Kluwer Academic Publishers.

Swinney, P. (2016). *Building the Northern Powerhouse: Lessons from the Rhine-Ruhr and Randstad*. London: Centre for Cities.

The Borderlands Initiative. (2017). The Borderlands proposition. Retrieved from http://www.borderlandsgrowth. com/Portals/0/Documents/Borderlands%20Proposition% 20September%202017.pdf?ver=2018-03-23-153451-327. Accessed on July 2019.

The Northern Powerhouse: One Agenda,One Economy,One North. A report on the Northern Transport Strategy March 2015. HM Government Transport for the North.

Tomanay, J. (2018, June 6). Great exhibition of what? Culture, region and development in England's north. *City Metric*. Retrieved from http://eprints.lse.ac.uk/88478/. Accessed on June 11, 2018.

Tomaney, J. (2018a). A Mess of Pottage? The North of Tyne Deal and the travails of devolution. Retrieved from http://blogs.lse.ac.uk/politicsandpolicy/ the-north-of-tyne-deal-and-the-travails-of-devolution/

Tomaney, J. (2018b, June 6). Great exhibition of what? Culture, region and development in England's north. *City Metric*. Retrieved from. Accessed on June 11, 2018.

Transport for the North's Northern Powerhouse Independent Economic Review (NPHIER). The Northern Powerhouse Independent Economic Review. Final Executive Summary 24th June 2011 SQW for TFN.

Travers, T. (2017, February 8). Power to the regions: Why more devolution makes sense. *The Guardian*. Retrieved from https://www.theguardian.com/ public-leaders-network/2017/feb/08/power-regions- more-devolution-cities-brexit

UK Government. (2017). *UK industrial strategy: Building a Britain fit for the Future*. London: HMSO.

Universities UK. (2014). The economic impact of the North East higher education sector. Retrieved from https://www.universitiesuk.ac.uk/policy-and-analysis/reports/Documents/2014/economic-impact-north-east.pdf. Accessed on June 29, 2019.

Universities UK. (2017a). The economic impact of higher education institution in England. Retrieved from https://www.universitiesuk.ac.uk/policy-and-analysis/reports/Documents/2014/the-impact-of-universities-on-the-uk-economy.pdf. Accessed on June 29, 2019.

Universities UK. (2017b). *What should be the governments priorities for exit negotiations and policy development to maximise the contribution of British universities to a successful and global UK?* London: Universities UK.

Universities UK. (2018). How can the government ensure universities are best placed to maximise their contribution to a successful and global UK post-EU Brexit? *Brexit Briefing*. Retrieved from https://www.universitiesuk.ac.uk/policy-and-analysis/reports/Documents/2018/brexit-briefing-march-18.pdf. Accessed on July 21, 2019.

Universities UK. (2019). The future of degree apprenticeships. *Retrieved from* https://www.universitiesuk.ac.uk/policy-and-analysis/reports/Documents/2019/future-degree-apprenticeships.pdf. Accessed on July 21, 2019.

University competition, student migration and regional economic differentials in the United Kingdom. (1991). *Higher Education, 22*(4), 351–370.

Urry, J. (2000). *Sociology beyond societies: Mobilities for the twenty-first century*. London: Routledge.

Urry, J. (2002). *The tourist gaze*. London: Sage.

Vyakarnam, S. (2009). *Educating the next wave of entrepreneurs: Unlocking entrepreneurial capabilities to meet the global challenges of the 21st century*. Switzerland: World Economic Forum.

Wang, N. (2000). *Tourism and modernity: A sociological analysis*. Oxford: Pergamon.

Well North. (2019). *Lasting change to our communities*. Well North. Retrieved from https://wellnorthenterprises. co.uk/wp-content/uploads/2019/05/Well-North-Legacy-Report-2019-FINAL.pdf

What Works Centre for Local Economic Growth. (2018). Developing Effective Local Industrial Strategies, WWCLEG, London. https://whatworksgrowth.org/public/ files/18-06-21_Designing_Effective_Local_Industrial_ Strategies.pdf

Wild, C., & Berger, D. (2016). The proposed teaching excellence framework (TEF) for UK universities. *International Journal of Teaching and Education*, 4(3), 33–50.

Williams, P. (2002). The Competent Boundary Spanner. *Public Administration*, 80(1), 103–124.

Wilson, T. (2012) *A review of business-university collaboration: the Wilson Review*. London: Crown Copyright.

Wilson, R., Maniatopoulos, G., Martin, M., & McLoughlin, I. (2012). Innovating relationships: Taking a co-productive approach to the shaping of telecare services for older people. *Information, Communication and Society*, 15(7), 1136–1163.

Woelfle, M., Olliaro, P., & Todd, M. H. (2011). Open science is a research accelerator. *Nature Chemistry*, 3(10), 75.

INDEX